Helion & Company Limited
Unit 8 Amherst Business Centre
Budbrooke Road
Warwick
CV34 5WE
England
Tel. 01926 499 619
Email: info@helion.co.uk
Website: www.helion.co.uk
Twitter: @helionbooks
Visit our blog http://blog.helion.co.uk/

Published by Helion & Company 2023
Designed and typeset by Farr out Publications, Wokingham, Berkshire
Cover designed by Paul Hewitt, Battlefield Design (www.battlefield-design.co.uk)

ISBN 978-1-804510-30-8

British Library Cataloguing-in-Publication Data
A catalogue record for this book is available from the British Library

We always welcome receiving book proposals from prospective authors.

CONTENTS

ABBREVIATIONS

ABFPM	Agrupacion de Batallones Felipe Peña Mendoza (Felipe Peña Mendoza Battalion Group or ABFPM
ANSESAL	Agencia Nacional de Servicios Especiales Salvadoreña (National Agency of Special Services of El Salvador)
ARENA	Alianza Republicana Nacionalista (Nationalist Republican Alliance or ARENA
BIRI	Batallones de Infantería de Reacción Inmediata (Immediate Reaction infantry Battalions)
BPR	Bloque Popular Revolucionario (People's Revolutionary Bloc)
BRAZ	Brígada Rafael Arce Zablah (Rafael Arce Zablah Brigade)
CG	Comandancia General (General Command)
CIA	Central Intelligence Agency
CICFA	Centro de Instruccion de Comandos de la Fuerza Armada (Armed Forces Commando Training Centre)
CIIFA	Centre de Instruccion de Ingenieros de la Fuerza Armada (Training Centre of Engineers of the Armed Forces)
CPM	Coordinadora Politico-Militar (Political-Military Coordination)
CRM	Coordinadora Revolucionaria de Masas (Revolutionary Mass Coordination)
DGI	Direccion de Inteligencia (Intelligence Directorate)
DM	Destacamento Militar (Military Detachment)
DRU	Direccion Revolucionaria Unificada (Unified Revolutionary Directorate)
ERP	Ejercito Revolucionario del Pueblo (People's Revolutionary Army)
FAL	Fuerzas Armadas de Liberacion (National Liberation Forces)
FAS	Fuerza Aérea Salvadoreña (Salvadoran Air Force)
FAES	Fuerzas Armadas de El Salvador (El Salvador Armed Forces)
FAPL	Fuerzas Armadas Populares de Liberacion (People's Armed Forces of Liberation)
FAPU	Frente de Acción Popular Unificada (Unified Popular Action Front)
FAR-LP	Fuerzas Armadas Revolucionarias de la Liberacion popular (Revolutionary Armed Forces of Popular Liberation)
FARN	Fuerzas Armadas de la Resistencia Nacional (Armed Forces of the National Resistance)
FDR	Frente Democrático Revolucionario (Revolutionary Democratic Front)
FECCAS	Federación Cristiana de Campesinos Salvadoreños (Christian Federation of Salvadoran Peasants or FECCAS
FES	Fuerzas Especiales Seleccionadas (Select Special Forces)
FMLN	Frente Farabundo Marti para la Liberacion Nacional (Farabundo Marti National Liberation Front)
FPL	Fuerzas Populares de Liberacion (Liberation People's Forces)
FUAR	Frente Unido de Acción Revolucionaria (United Front of Revolutionary Action)
GARS	Grupos de Acción Revolucionaria (Revolutionary Action Groups)
GN	Guardia Nacional (National Guard)
JRG	Junta Revolucionaria de Gobierno (Revolutionary Government Junta)
KGB	Komitet gossoudarstvennoï bezopasnosti (Committee for State Security)
km	kilometre
MNR	Movimiento Nacional Revolucionario (Revolutionary National Movement or MNR
NCO	Non-commissioned officer
OAS	Organisation of American States
ORDEN	Organizacion Democratica Nacionalista (National Democratic Organisation)
PCS	Partido Comunista Salvadoreño (Salvadoran Communist Party)
PLO	Palestine Liberation Organisation
PN	Policia Nacional (National Police)
PAR	Partido de Acción Renovadora (Renewal Action Party)
PCN	Partido de Conciliacion Nacional (National Conciliation Party)
PDC	Partido Democrata Cristiano (Democratic Christian Party)
PH	Policia de Hacienda (Treasury Police)
PRUD	Partido Revolucionario de Unificacion Democratica (Revolutionary Party of Democratic Unification)
PRTC	Partido Revolucionario de los Trabajadores Centroamericanos (Revolutionary Party of Central America Workers)
RN	Resistencia Nacional (National Resistance)
SI	Socialist International
SOA	School of Americas
UCA	Universidad Centroamericana (Central American University)
UGB	Union Guerrera Blanca (White Warriors Union)
UNO	Union Nacional Opositora (National Opposition Union)
US$	United States Dollar

ACKNOWLEDGEMENTS

This book would not have been able to be written without the support, encouragement and help of Tom Cooper and Bill Norton. I want to thank them for this and also for their patience and benevolence towards me. I also thank Albert Grandolini who had the kindness to share the photos of his collection.

INTRODUCTION

During the 1980s, El Salvador received disproportionate attention given the modest size of its territory and population. The scene of a civil war between Left and Right, the ideological conflict in this small Central American republic has featured political actors from all over the world willing to engage in one way or another, in the socio-political drama that Salvadorans were experiencing and which was part of the global struggle between communism and capitalism.

Yet the history of El Salvador has been shaped by violence from the day the Conquistador Pedro de Alvarado gave his name to this small Central American country, up until the gang wars that ravage this country today. The political, social and economic violence, which accelerated during the 1970s, culminating in a civil war in the early 1980s, was the real trigger and engine of a conflict that lasted more than 12 years. It was also part of a Latin America that was not stingy with armed conflicts after 1945 and the one that affected El Salvador in the 1980s as an echo of the revolutionary cycle inaugurated in Cuba in 1959.

Nevertheless, the Salvadoran conflict had some singularities that distinguish it from those that struck Latin America during the Cold War. In the words of Charles E. Spencer, El Salvador saw 'the best militarily developed insurgent movement in the history of the American continent'.[1] This was in a country that all military specialists considered unsuitable for guerrilla warfare. The *Frente Farabundo Marti para la Liberacion Nacional* (Farabundo Marti National Liberation Front or FMLN) simply failed to survive for many long years; it almost won and, if it failed to win, it was not defeated by arms, despite Washington's support for the Salvadoran government.

This was a new peculiarity of the Salvadoran conflict. If, unlike the Sandinista guerrillas, the FMLN did not seize power by force, it was because of the scale of the American intervention, which resulted in both massive economic and military aid and the application methods of counter-insurgency warfare in a small country hitherto ignored by the American superpower.

Resulting from an internal crisis, the Salvadoran conflict appeared as the acme of a form of war which punctuated the history of the twentieth century; called revolutionary or popular war by one camp and counter-insurgency war by the other camp. The FMLN was based on the military experiences of the revolutionary movement combining insurrection, urban guerrilla warfare and a protracted people's war whilst the Americans implemented strategies resulting from the experience of the British in Malaysia, the French in Indochina and Algeria and their intervention in Vietnam.

If Salvadoran civil war – which broke out when the Cold War was revived following the election of Ronald Reagan and ended when the USSR no longer existed and the Cold War had become a closed chapter in history – was therefore rich for the study of military history, it should nevertheless not make us forget that it caused the death of more than 70,000 people, or 1.4 percent of the population of El Salvador.

1
EL SALVADOR FROM SPANISH CONQUEST TO THE DAWN OF CIVIL WAR

El Salvador appears on a map of Central America as a small state bordering the Pacific Ocean, sandwiched between Guatemala to the west and Honduras to the north and east. It is separated from Nicaragua only by a narrow strip of land of 25 kilometres, outlet of Honduras on the Pacific in the Gulf of Fonseca. Three large geographical areas characterise this country, a narrow plain that runs along almost the entire Pacific coast, dominated by a volcanic chain crossing its heart and extended by an area of high rugged mountains inside the territory to the border north with Honduras.

The tropical climate and volcanic soil make El Salvador fertile ground for coffee plantations, the country's main source of wealth for a century and a half, which cover vast areas of steep volcanic slopes. At the end of the twentieth century, the coastal plain increased its economic importance when the government cleared land for cattle grazing and the cultivation of cotton and sugar cane. The mountains of the north-east, meanwhile, are populated by poor farmers living on the margins of economic life. Nevertheless, the main division of the country results from the presence of one of the largest rivers in Central America, the Lempa River, which crosses El Salvador from north to south. The two large bridges built over this river during the twentieth century serve as fragile links between two different regions since the eastern part of the country, which is more rural, is less economically developed.

Demographically, in 1980, with approximately 5 million inhabitants in a territory of 21,393km^2, El Salvador was the most densely populated country in Latin America with 226 inhabitants per square kilometre. Unlike other regions of this continent, its population was homogeneous, made up of 90 percent Métis, nine percent White and one percent Native Americans (Amerindians) who did not distinguish any striking cultural differences.

From Colonisation to Independence

It is this geographically contrasting territory that Spanish ships, coming from Panama, discovered in 1522. Two years later, troops coming from New Spain, present-day Mexico, commanded by Pedro de Alvarado, embarked on the conquest of Central America. In June 1524, the first Spaniards reached a territory called Cuzcatlán by the native inhabitants and which Alvarado renamed San Salvador, 'the Holy Saviour', in reference to Jesus Christ. The Spaniards encountered strong resistance which forced them to retreat to Guatemala and they needed two military campaigns in 1525 and 1528 to defeat the Amerindians. The conquistadores were quickly followed by civilians who settled in localities that would become the largest cities in the country, San Salvador created in 1525, San Miguel in 1530 and Trinidad in 1533.

Spaniards did not settle in an empty country. The Amerindian population, which they called the Pipiles, was linked, by language and culture, to the Aztec civilisation of Mexico. The Pipiles, who developed an agricultural and merchant society, built cities and roads and possessed a written language, fiercely opposed the Europeans. Thus, it took nearly 15 years for the Conquistadors to control the country.

Faced with the impossibility of extracting precious metals that were almost non-existent in El Salvador, the Spaniards opted for the exploitation of the only possible resource, the ground. After their victory, they established their administration and offered land to settlers who were cultivated by the Pipiles and subjected to forced labour. Colonial society thus developed an export economy of agricultural products, notably cocoa and indigo, whilst the Amerindians were decimated by disease. To ensure the functioning of this economic system based on forced labour, militias were founded to suppress possible indigenous rebellions, collected taxes and ensured the permanence and obedience of the workforce.[1]

As in all of Latin America, the colonial system began to crumble in the early nineteenth century as Spain's power declined. In 1811, there was a first uprising in El Salvador demanding autonomy, but it was violently suppressed. Three years later a new revolt inaugurated a war of independence that lasted nearly seven years. On 15 September 1821, the colonies of the General Captaincy of Guatemala declared their independence from Spain. Faced with the attempts of Agustín de Iturbide, the ruler of Mexico, to annex the former colonies of Central America to his country, El Salvador, Honduras, Guatemala, Nicaragua and Costa Rica unified within the United Provinces of Central America in 1823.[2] This year saw also the birth of the Salvadoran Army, formed by the union of several cavalry corps fighting against Mexican attacks.

Divided between Conservatives and Liberals, the United Provinces gradually disintegrated under the pressure of constant struggles. Finally, the five states abandoned their efforts to unite, and each declared their independence, which El Salvador did in January 1841. Independence did not put an end to the problems facing the country, in particular poverty and discrimination against the natives. In 1833, the Nonualcos, Amerindian populations living around Zacatecoluca and San Vicente, revolted under the leadership of Aquino and reinforcements were needed to restore order and prevent the rebels from controlling the whole country.[3]

In the years following the Nonualco rebellion, a new export culture emerged in El Salvador. As early as 1840, high-quality coffee was produced profitably on the volcanic slopes of the country. In 1864, whilst the value of coffee production exceeded the decline in indigo revenues, large amounts of land still remained in the hands of indigenous communities who practised food crops on small plots under communal control. For the government, obsessed with the need to increase coffee production, this situation represented an obstacle to progress. In 1881 and 1882, the Legislative Assembly passed a series of laws abolishing communal land tenure and establishing mechanisms for allocating such land to anyone who would use it for growing coffee and other export crops. It was at this time that a small group of large landowners formed. The integration of El Salvador into the world economy through coffee production allowed the consolidation of this oligarchy of producers who gradually gained political power, in particular through the financial support they provided to the government. This allowed them to impose laws governing daily labour in agriculture and prohibiting the organisation of agricultural workers. Coffee culture became the basis of economic and political power.[4]

The conquest of Central America by the Spaniards was particularly brutal and encountered resistance from the local populations. It thus took several years for the Conquistadors to conquer the territory of present-day El Salvador. (Author's Collection)

The grip of the coffee producers on the government also had consequences in the military field. Unlike the rest of the region, the Salvadorans had a disciplined army in the mid-nineteenth century made up of infantry, cavalry and artillery. Under pressure from the coffee oligarchy, these *Fuerzas Armadas de El Salvador* (El Salvador Armed Forces or FAES) provided less defence against an external enemy than internal security against the frequent revolts of indigenous peasants. In return, the oligarchy protected the

The development of coffee production in the nineteenth century profoundly transformed El Salvador, giving it the political, economic and social features that it retained until the 1980s. The large landowners were the real holders of power and imposed their will on a harshly exploited landless peasantry. (Author's Collection)

interests of the military and guaranteed the expansion of the FAES. They created also, in 1912, the *Guardia Nacional* (National Guard or GN) to ensure the security of the coffee plantations and suppress peasant protests.[5]

El Salvador experienced a period of political stability during the years 1870–1927, essentially marked by the absence of change in the unequal social structure and the liberal policy of the country.

The Presidency of Maximiliano Hernandez Martinez

In 1927, Pio Romero Bosque was elected president of El Salvador. Considering the growth of popular organisations throughout the 1920s, he sought to integrate them into the political game. For this, he promised holding free elections and criticised the systematic repression of workers.[6] This democratic opening quickly came up against the crisis of 1929 which hit the Salvadoran economy hard. Thus, between 1928 and 1931, the international price of coffee fell by 54 percent.[7] Food supplies, which depended on imports due to the expansion of coffee monoculture, were tight. The coffee oligarchy reacted by drastically reducing the wages of workers, many of whom found themselves unemployed. Craftsmen went bankrupt and civil servants also saw their wages drop.[8]

Politically, the presidential elections of 1931 were the first free elections in El Salvador. They were won by Arturo Araujo who was supported by a coalition of students, labour activists and landowners stricken by the Great Depression.[9] However, these elections came as discontent grew in a country reeling from the global economic crisis. From 1928, the influence of the communists increased sharply in western El Salvador, especially among peasants and rural workers hit by falling wages who launched strikes in 1931 and moved closer to the *Partido Comunista Salvadoreño* (Salvadoran Communist Party or PCS), founded in 1930 and led by Agustín Farabundo Marti.[10]

Although President Araujo began by suppressing workers' and peasants' demonstrations, he remained faithful to his reformist strategy and proposed to authorise the participation of the PCS in the municipal elections of December 1931. This concession caused the discontent of the oligarchy and to a greater extent, the FAES. Araujo was overthrown in a coup on 2 December 1931 and his former vice president and Minister of War, General Maximiliano Hernandez Martinez, took power.[11]

Augustin Farabundo Marti Rodriguez was a revolutionary who at the end of the 1920s was a member of the Anti-Imperialist League of Americas where he met the Nicaraguan Augusto Sandino. He joined the PCS and became one of the leaders. He was sentenced to death and executed after the failure of the 1932 uprising and became a martyr for the Left movement. (Author's Collection)

For their part, the communists organised the workers and peasants who demanded the return of the communal lands confiscated from the Amerindians and the 8 hour working day for all workers. Martinez's refusal to let the elected communists sit in the municipalities where they were elected, added to the deterioration of the economic situation and pushed the PCS to prepare an

With his seizure of power by a coup in December 1931 and the massacre of communist insurgents in 1932, General Maximiliano Hernandez Martinez inaugurated 50 years of military power in El Salvador. (Author's Collection)

insurrection. However, the authorities were made aware of this plan and arrested Marti. The poorly planned Izalcó peasant uprising, which began on 22 January 1932, was a rout for the coffee workers who were crushed by government troops in just three days. Between 8,000 and 10,000 people were massacred, the vast majority being indigenous peasants.[12] Salvadorans called this episode the *Matanza*, a stronger term than massacre which reflected the collective trauma it caused. The peasant unions were dissolved and Marti and other communist leaders were shot, becoming the figureheads and martyrs of the Salvadoran revolutionary movement.

With the *Matanza* and the coming to power of General Martinez, the link between the landed elite and the FAES was reinforced and sealed the nature of the regime for the years to come, based on the shared fear of a new communist revolt. From 1931 and for half a century, the military, supported by the oligarchy, remained in power through repression, electoral fraud and coups. Thus, during the period 1931–1970, eight of the nine presidents of the country were soldiers. The sole civilian president ruled only four months until replaced by military.[13]

Martinez ruled the country through repression, forcing the opposition into exile or underground. He moved quickly to consolidate his power and put in place economic reforms which, together with the wage cuts imposed after the *Matanza*, ensured the survival of the coffee oligarchy. Nevertheless, he also initiated social reforms in favour of the poor, such as the establishment of a social security system or the recognition of trade unions, with the aim of avoiding uprisings like that of 1932.[14]

Martinez ended up angering the oligarchy when he tried to raise export taxes and showed his desire to stay in power after 1944, again breaking the Constitution. Although a coup attempt against him failed, growing discontent and a general strike eventually forced him to resign on 8 May 1944. His successor, General Andrés Ignacio Menéndez was overthrown after 5 months in power to be replaced by the Director of the *Policia Nacional* (National Police or PN), Colonel Osmin Aguirre y Salinas. He ruled the country until the elections of January 1945 which saw the victory of General Salvador Castañeda Castro, however, on 14 December 1948, when he illegally tried to extend his term, Castañeda was overthrown in a bloodless coup led by young reformist soldiers.[15]

Between Military Dictatorship and Economic Growth

The 1948 coup marked a new stage in the evolution of the place of the FAES in the life of El Salvador. The latter declared they wanted to establish a democratic regime where citizens could freely choose their leaders. This desire changed the perception that the population had of the FAES, which were beginning to be considered as the guardians of law enforcement and national sovereignty and not as a private army at the service of the oligarchy.[16] However, the FAES, which governed the country until the elections of March 1950, always avoided challenging the power of this oligarchy and initiating fundamental reforms. In 1949, a law even banned Left-wing parties whilst, to consolidate their power, the military created their own Party, the *Partido Revolucionario de Unificacion Democratica* (Revolutionary Party of Democratic Unification or PRUD).[17]

Major Oscar Osorio was the PRUD presidential candidate in 1950 and won the elections. He initiated a modernising project that wanted to make the FAES both the guarantors of change and the guardians of the new aspirations of society. A new Constitution was promulgated in 1950 which gave a new role to the State, that of promoting national development and ensuring social well-being. The government's desire for reform nevertheless had its limits as during the 1956 presidential elections, the PRUD candidate, Lieutenant Colonel José Maria Lemus, obtained 93 percent of the votes in elections rigged by soldiers who monitored the ballots and the vote count. Nonetheless, despite these electoral frauds, the PRUD expressed the will of the FAES to promote a new elite in the shadow of a State which wished to free itself from the tutelage of the oligarchy.[18]

A further drop in export coffee prices and the enactment of an electoral law that prevented the existence of an opposition, quickly undermined the weak popularity of Lemus's government. For its part, the influence of the Cuban Revolution stimulated the organisation of several demonstrations calling for the resignation of the president and the establishment of a democratic system. The government responded by stepping up repression, banning free speech and imprisoning any political dissidents. For the oligarchy, economic development was not possible in such an environment whilst the nascent middle class felt threatened and the FAES were no longer willing to support such an authoritarian president.[19]

A coup overthrew Lemus on 26 October 1960. The new civil-military Junta that took power included Fabio Castillo, a professor who sympathised with the Cuban Revolution. His presence convinced the economic elite and the most conservative military, that the government was influenced by communism. Once again, the FAES overthrew the Junta on 25 January 1961. This Coup provoked the anger of civilians who, during a demonstration in San Salvador, were violently repressed by the police and the GN. Although certain centrist and Left-wing political groups began to organise themselves for the 1962 elections, they could not prevent the victory of Lieutenant Colonel Rivera, candidate of the *Partido de Conciliacion Nacional* (National Conciliation Party or PCN) which replaced the PRUD of the previous period.[20]

Although the opposition was marginalised, it had representatives thanks to the modification of the electoral system carried out by Rivera which allowed proportional suffrage in Parliament. The *Partido Demócrata Cristiano* (Democratic Christian Party or PDC) appeared to be the great beneficiary of this reform. Founded in 1960, responding to the modernising aspirations of the urban middle classes, it quickly acquired the status of the main opposition party. Two smaller parties, the communist-dominated *Partido de Accion Renovadora* (Renewal Action Party or PAR), and the social-

President Oscar Osorio, who was President of El Salvador from 1950 to 1956, pursued a policy of reform, with the aim of improving the living conditions of the population whilst harshly repressing all forms of opposition to military power. (Author's Collection)

democratic *Movimiento Nacional Revolucionario* (Revolutionary National Movement or MNR), led by Guillermo Ungo, completed the protest horizon. As with the unions, their existence remained subject to the goodwill of the military authorities.

In the 1964 elections, the first under the new electoral system, the PDC won 13 seats whilst the PCN retained the majority. One of the PDC founders, José Napoleon Duarte Fuentes, also won the mayoralty of San Salvador in 1964. His politics allowed him to be re-elected twice in a row as mayor of the capital and to gain a base of support, especially within the middle class. The successes of his municipal administration made him a figure of national importance.[21]

During the years of PCN domination, the FAES continued to govern El Salvador and served the interests of the economic elite. Under a democratic mask, with the authorisation of a moderate opposition which could participate in the elections and the prohibition of those who refused the alliance between the oligarchy and the FAES, the military retained control of the country. The PCN won the elections, thanks to massive fraud, throughout the 1960s. In 1967, its candidate, Colonel Fidel Sanchez Hernandez, was elected President of the Republic.[22]

Although the political system remained dominated by the FAES, El Salvador, like the rest of Central America, experienced significant changes after 1945. The population increased from 1.8 million inhabitants in the 1940s to 2.5 million in 1961, this boom mainly benefiting cities. Above all, the state increased its role in economic and social life. Huge investments in the country's infrastructure were made and the manufacturing industry grew rapidly thanks to the regional economic integration through the Central American Common Market founded in 1962.[23]

The State also created social security, promulgated a labour code in 1949 and developed educational and health action policies. Nevertheless, this modernisation did not erase the great social inequalities that divided Salvadoran society. Wage rates were still low whilst profit rates remained very high, and the expansion of cotton and sugar cane production along the coastal plain and in the rich northern valleys, further concentrated land ownership among a few hands. At the end of the 1960s, 60 percent of the rural population had no land, whilst 64 percent of the country's land belonged to only four percent of owners.[24] In response, thousands of poor Salvadoran peasants crossed the border into Honduras where land was relatively abundant, sowing the seeds of the 1969 military conflict.

The Soccer War and its Aftermath

The 'Soccer War' between El Salvador and Honduras had its roots in the economic differences between the two countries. Honduras was larger, less populated and less developed than its neighbour. El Salvador's population density, one of the highest in Central America, for decades found an outlet in immigration to Honduras. Thus, at the end of the 1960s, approximately 300,000 Salvadorans lived in Honduras. In this country, their presence was increasingly badly perceived, especially since El Salvador's industry progressed whilst the industry of Honduras was stagnating and which the latter, supported less and less.[25] Tensions between the two countries increased when Honduran President Lopez Arellano decided to expel Salvadoran peasants.

The closure of the border by Honduras in June 1969 quickly caused an industrial crisis in El Salvador and the rise of unemployment. It was in this context that, during a series of qualifying matches for the Soccer World Cup between El Salvador and Honduras, violent clashes broke out between supporters, aggravating tensions.

Large scale military operations began when El Salvador sent 8,000 troops to attack on 14 July as the *Fuerza Aérea Salvadoreña* (Salvadoran Air Force or FAS) struck major cities and Air Bases in Honduras. The Salvadoran Ground Army was superior in numbers with 8,000 soldiers and 105mm artillery pieces, whilst its Honduran counterpart was weaker, comprising only 2,500 soldiers armed with old American rifles. The Honduran Air Force, on the contrary, with 23 Corsair type combat aircraft, was superior to the FAS which had only 11 Mustang and Corsair type combat aircraft. The FAES attacked along the main road joining the two countries and against the Honduran islands in the Gulf of Fonseca. At first, they advanced rapidly and by the evening of 15 July, the provincial capital of Nueva Ocotepeque was taken. However, the Honduran Air Force succeeded in putting the FAS out of action and destroying the FAES ammunition and fuel depots, forcing the latter to immobility.[26]

After four days of fighting, on 19 July, under pressure from the international community and the Organization of American States (OAS), the Salvadorans withdrew their troops. The war caused 3,000 deaths and some 15,000 injuries. Nearly 50,000 people lost their homes and lands whilst many villages were destroyed.[27]

Salvadoran M3 Stuart tank rolls through the streets of Nueva Ocotepeque during the 1969 W ar against Honduras. (Albert Grandolini Collection)

El Salvadoran soldiers during the Hundred Hours War. (Albert Grandolini Collection)

The price of military victory for El Salvador was a large scale diplomatic, economic and social crisis. Internationally, it found himself isolated for having attacked Honduras, whilst economically, the war marked the end of the Central American Common Market, a favourable target as the country had to absorb some 100,000 expatriates from Honduras.[28] The debate on the unequal distribution of land also returned to the forefront and with it, the demand for agrarian reform which became the essential issue of the legislative elections of 1970 and the presidential elections of 1972.[29]

For these elections, the political opposition was represented by the PDC and the PAR, two parties slightly to the Left, promising reforms in the distribution of land and which received the support of the lower classes, in particular rural workers. To counter their influence, President Sanchez used his popularity after the 1969 war to enact land and education reforms despite opposition from the oligarchy.[30] The latter blocked their application before they could make any changes, whilst the defeat of the opposition in the 1970 elections convinced the PDC to do something different to have a chance of winning the 1972 presidential elections.

The PDC, located at the Centre of the political spectrum, became the main adversary of the PCN. For the 1972 elections, PDC formed with the Nationalist Democratic Union and the MNR the coalition *Union Nacional Opositora* (National Union of the Opposition or UNO) which presented Napoleon Duarte as its candidate. Even though the other parties were more Left-wing than the PDC, UNO's electoral platform was moderate and called for measured reforms and respect for private property.

The population, faced with the choice between the PCN candidate, Colonel Arturo Armando Molina and the ultra-conservative Medrano, supported Duarte and the UNO. However, the February 1972 elections were one of the worst cases of voter fraud in Salvadoran history. Whilst observers agreed that the UNO won the elections, the publication of the results was suspended before the National Assembly, dominated by the PCN, choose Molina as winner.[31]

A group of military officers and PCN members shocked by electoral fraud, revolted on 25 March 1972. Led by Colonel Benjamin Mejia Gonzalez, who commanded the Artillery regiment, the officers entered the presidential residence and arrested President Sanchez. At the same time, the Artillery regiment bombed the GN barracks and also the FAS air base which remained loyal to the president. Supporters of Mejia, joined by the 1st Infantry Brigade, based in San Salvador, also took control of the country's communications network.[32] Duarte rallied behind the coup and spoke on radio broadcasts asking the population to support it. The Coup was nevertheless quickly and brutally crushed by the GN and the FAS. Mustangs and Corsairs, under fire from anti-aircraft batteries, bombarded the San Carlos barracks and the surroundings of the University of El Salvador. Duarte was arrested and sent into exile in Venezuela.[33]

The Mejia's Coup represented a dramatic turning point for El Salvador. Since 1932, the FAES had dominated the country as part of an alliance with the oligarchy, ensuring that the latter maintained its economic hegemony. At the same time, the military were also reformers, which allowed them to enjoy the support of the middle class and not remain dependent on the oligarchy. This system was

El Salvadoran M3 Stuart parading through San Salvador with a captured Honduran flag. (Albert Grandolini Collection)

challenged by the ability of the UNO to win the support of the middle and lower classes in elections and the use of fraud eventually blew it apart. The Coup indeed showed that this solution divided the FAES whilst its failure led to the end of the UNO as an intermediary between the Left and the Right. The opposition lost hope of gaining power through elections, which pushed part of the population to consider more radical actions.[34]

The Birth of Left-wing Armed Groups

At the beginning of the 1970s, the private and public universities of El Salvador, whose number of students grew from 3,000 to 30,000 in a decade, became hotbeds of anti-government agitation.[35] Revolutionary culture predominated in Latin America and the triumph of the Cuban Revolution was, in the eyes of thousands of young Latin Americans, an example of socio-political change.

The universities were transformed into places of debates and confrontations between the different Marxist-Leninist movements and the PCS. This was where Left-wing organisations appeared which, faced with the absence of a democratic system, sought other more effective forms of organisation, combining armed struggle and mass organisation. Nevertheless, in the early 1970s El Salvador seemed an unlikely place for a guerrilla. The memory of the 1932 *Matanza* still haunted the memories of the Left and the defeats of several Latin American revolutionary movements pushed the small PCS to maintain a legalist strategy.[36]

Since 1932, the PCS had continued to survive in a semi-clandestine manner. At the end of the 1950s, it began to prepare for the armed struggle by creating, in June 1961, the *Frente Unido de Accion Revolucionaria* (United Front for Revolutionary Action or FUAR). In 1962, the police managed to dismantle this organisation and arrested its leader, Schafik Handal. Finally, the FUAR was dissolved in 1965. More than the action of the police, it was the Soviet refusal of armed struggle in Latin America in favour of the electoral struggle that determined the position of the PCS. This did not mean that the communists renounced the creation of military formations since they maintained a Military Commission and set up self-defence groups, but which were only responsible for defending the great popular mobilisations and the Party's leaders.[37]

Faced with the legalism of the PCS, a small group of Salvadoran communists left the Party and formed the *Fuerzas Populares de Liberacion Farabundo Marti* (Farabundo Mari People's Liberation Forces or FPL) on 1st April 1970. Its leader was Salvador Cayetano Carpio, who from 1964 to 1970, was the General Secretary of the PCS. Carpio, already opposed to communist support for the 1969 war against Honduras, believed it was time to prepare for the revolution in El Salvador, a revolution which, on the Vietnamese model, involved armed struggle.[38]

If on 4 April 1971, militants of the FPL Central Command confronted the GN, it was not until 22 April 1972, when a bomb exploded in front of the Argentine embassy, that the FPL made their public appearance. They then developed in different sectors (particularly in universities) and their privileged field of action was in the cities where they formed guerrilla commandos of five members. In 1974 there were already about 60 fighters in the city of San Salvador alone. On 6 March 1974, five commandos, in effect 25 fighters, tried to kidnap the President of the Central Electoral Council, but the latter was absent, and the FPL militants finally set fire to the building after having killed two GNs and captured five others who were then released. The FPL also sought to settle in the countryside and it was through contacts with progressive priests that they established themselves in the north and centre of the country, particularly in the Chalatenango department.[39]

Salvador Cayetano Carpio, alias Commander Marcial, broke with the PCS legalism and founded the FPL in 1970, the objective of which was to seize power through armed struggle. (Author's Collection)

From 1974, the FPL established relations with Cuba but especially, with North Vietnam. Inside El Salvador, the commandos were regrouped in the capital to form the first column of urban guerrillas, then at the end of 1975, militias were organised. In 1977, the FPL set up an Intelligence Commission, a Strategic Commission and also a medical structure. Thanks to this organisation, they carried out various military actions, bombings, kidnappings and executions of politicians, businessmen and high officials.[40]

In 1970, other PCS dissidents and young people from the most radical wing of the PDC formed *El Grupo* (The Group), led by Héctor Alejandro Rivas Mira and Vladimir Rogel Umaña.[41] This group was separated from the FPL on a major strategic issue. Unlike the latter, who was in favour of a protracted rural war, for El Grupo it was possible to conquer power through urban guerrilla warfare and insurrection. On this point and as shown by his first actions, it was inspired by the success of the Tupamaros of Uruguay and the Argentinian Montoneros. On 11 February 1971, it kidnapped businessman Ernesto Regalado Dueña and then executed him. On 2 March 1972, it shot two members of the GN to steal their G-3 rifles.[42]

El Grupo quickly collaborated with other close organisations such as the *Comandos Organizadores del Pueblo* (People's Organising Commandos) led by Arce Zablah and Rodrigo Solorzano, but also a group of very radicalised young people from the PCS and led by Vladimir Rogel. The grouping of these different organisations formed the *Ejercito Revolucionario del Pueblo* (People's Revolutionary Army or ERP), officially founded on 2 March 1972. Through Father Miguel Ventura, Rafael Arce Zablah encountered Catholic communities in the regions of Torola, El Rosario and San Fernando in Morazan where ERP began to be established in 1974. From 1972 to 1975, the ERP carried out several kidnappings and military actions, dynamite attacks against police stations, small garrisons or businesses, arms thefts, assassinations of GNs and police officers to seize their weapons. These actions allowed them to gain notoriety and raise money through ransoms.[43]

Since its inception, the ERP had prioritised military action, driving a wedge in the organisation between those who believed the time had come for armed insurrection and those who, like the internationally acclaimed poet Roque Dalton, wanted to build political organisations to complement military action. In 1973, supporters of this last tendency left the ERP to create the *Organizacion Revolucionaria de los Trabajadores* (Workers' Revolutionary Organisation) led by Fabio Castillo which gave birth to the *Partido Revolucionario de los Trabajadores Centroamericanos* (Revolutionary Party of the Central American Workers or PRTC). The controversy culminated with the assassination of Dalton and Armando Arteaga on 10 May 1975, perpetrated on the orders of the ERP General Staff, under the accusation of espionage for both the CIA, the KGB and the Cuban secret services but in truth, to stifle the internal debate.

The same day, Ernesto Jovel, Eduardo Sancho and Lil Milagro Ramirez announced their departure from the organisation which remained isolated until 1980. Finally, in 1977, with Villalobos at its head, the ERP decided to have an organisation, the *Ligua Popular-28 Febrero* (People's League 28 February or LP-28) as well as a political arm, the *Partido de la Revolucion Salvadoreña* (Salvadoran Revolution Party).[44]

The leaders who left the ERP after the murder of Dalton, created the *Resistencia Nacional* (National Resistance or RN) in 1975. They were joined by the *Frente Obrero Campesino* (Peasant Worker Front), strongly established in the Cerro de Guazapa. The RN created a military group called the *Fuerzas Armades de la Resistencia Nacional*

The strategy of the FPL was based on the theory of protracted people's war according to the Maoist model. The organisation, borne in the cities, therefore took care to establish itself in the countryside during the 1970s, which it managed to do in the rural areas of the Chalatenango department. (Albert Grandolini Collection)

A demonstration of the *Bloque Popular Revolucionario* in a neighbourhood of San Salvadot. This mass organisation linked to the FPL, aggregated the demands and discontent of the population against the military power. (Albert Grandolini Collection)

(National Resistance Armed Forces or FARN) which was structured around the *Grupos de Autodefensa Militar de Masas* (Mass Military Self-Defence Groups).[45]

In 1971, another armed group began to form which would later give birth to the PRTC. It was made up of radical university students who wanted a socialist revolution throughout Central America. From its creation, it became closer to the ERP with whom it carried out military actions in 1972 before diverging.[46] In 1976, it created a military structure, the *Comandos Armados de Liberacion* (Armed Commandos of Liberation), which, under the direction of Roberto Galeano, were made up of small, highly compartmentalised groups of a few individuals.[47] It was finally, on 2 February 1977, that the

PRTC was officially born, bringing together dissidents from the RN and the PCS, as well as Salvadoran exiles in Costa Rica.

Whilst numerous, the guerrilla organisations that emerged in the 1970s, were militarily weak. Facundo Guardado says they 'were small – each consisted of a few dozen members. They were lightly armed: a carbine, a pistol, hardly anything really'.[48]

Their importance was above all, proportional to the failures of the legal opposition which fed their ranks. Their influence was all the greater when they infiltrated and took the direction of student organisations, professional unions or civil associations whose actions they articulated and coordinated. The idea of these gatherings of organisations working in different sectors came from the experience of Vietnam, where the formation of a broad national liberation front was the key to uniting the population under the hegemony of the revolutionaries.

The *Frente de Accion Popular Unificada* (Unified Popular Action Front or FAPU) was born in June 1974 under the aegis of the RN. The *Bloque Popular Revolucionario* (People's Revolutionary Bloc or BPR) was founded in 1975 and linked to the FPL. In 1977, the ERP formed the LP-28 and the PRTC the *Movimiento de Liberacion Popular* (People's Liberation Movement) in 1976. Through these mass organisations that framed thousands of people, the guerrilla organisations tried to incite the politicisation of the population through the choice of mobilisation strategies that provoked repression.[49]

Faced with the appearance of Left-wing armed groups and their popular organisations, the frightened oligarchy responded by financing death squads made up of military and former soldiers. In the public arena, they appeared under different names and used the media to express the ideas of the radical Right. They specialised in the kidnapping of opponents of the regime, followed by the abandonment of the corpse a few hours later, mutilated or with various traces of brutal torture.[50] Salvadoran society was thus, increasingly divided and polarised by the action of each camp.

The Catholic Church went into Opposition

The social disorder that has hit El Salvador since 1972 was such that it pushed the Catholic Church to take a stand. In a country where 81 percent of the population was Catholic, the Church had always supported the government and the oligarchy. Things changed in the 1970s when some of them turned to the opposition and demanded changes to solve the country's problems.

This evolution was part of a broader development of Catholicism after the Second Vatican Council of 1965 and the declaration of Pope John XXIII announcing that the Church had to go beyond spiritual education and became the defender of the community. This declaration was followed by a conference in Medellin, Colombia, in 1968, where the bishops of Latin America called on the Church to 'defend the rights of the oppressed'.[51]

In El Salvador, priests who visited small rural communities, preached that people were not condemned to poverty by God. They also politicised the population by organising Basic Christian Communities whose purpose was to study the Bible, to promote joint work and the sharing of responsibilities. This allowed the peasants to become aware of their plight and to demand agrarian reform, higher wages and better working conditions. The *Federación Cristiana de Campesinos Salvadoreños* (Christian Federation of Salvadoran Peasants or FECCAS), founded in 1964 by the Church, contested the prerogatives of the oligarchy.[52] Under the leadership of the priests, strikes or occupations of land were carried out from

The Archbishop of San Salvador, Oscar Romero was both the symbol of opposition to the military regime and the hope for a peaceful exit from the deep crisis in his country. (Author's Collection)

1973 as well as demonstrations for the increase in the wages of the day labourers.

FECCAS was strengthened with the announcement of an agrarian reform promised by President Molina in 1976. Nearly 61,000 hectares had to be nationalised in order to calm the rise of unrest.[53] But the Minister of Defence, Carlos Romero, threatened to carry out a coup if this reform succeeded. The failure of this reform and military repression during strikes and demonstrations helped to radicalise FECCAS. The ecclesiastical authorities on their side protested against the level of violence of the State.

The oligarchy's response was to criticise the priests for organising the people against the government whose legitimacy it was eroding. The *Unión Guerrera Blanca* (White Warriors Union or UGB), a death squad, began distributing pamphlets declaring 'Be a patriot. Kill a priest'.[54] The latter became a target for Right-wing paramilitary groups. Between January and July 1977, two priests were killed, two tortured, one beaten, two imprisoned and four threatened with death. The assassination of Father Rutilio Grande on 17 March 1977 had important implications.[55]

With Grande's death, the Catholic Church overwhelmingly protested official repression. The archbishop of El Salvador, Oscar Romero, became a vocal critic of the government. His weekly mass, broadcasted on YSAX, the Church's radio station, became the most listened to programme in El Salvador. Romero not only read the scriptures, but he also commented on political subjects and attacked the government and the death squads. The Right understood that he was seeking to mobilise the people against government violence and responded with bombings that hit the radio station.

The withdrawal of the agrarian reform projects promised by President Molina and the absence of the possibility of political alternation in a climate of increasingly violent repression, increased the discontent of the Church, the UNO, Leftist armed groups and their mass organisations. But this opposition was divided. If the Church and the UNO advocated the return to democracy and elections, the revolutionary groups called for following the insurrectionary path.

The Crisis of the Military Regime

The increase in the level of violence plunged El Salvador into a serious economic and social crisis. It was in this situation that,

Throughout 1979, El Salvador experienced increasing violence. The repression of the security forces responded to popular demonstrations increasingly supported by armed groups of Left-wing organisations. (Albert Grandolini Collection)

for the presidential elections of 1977, General Carlos Humberto Romero was appointed by the PCN to succeed Molina. Romero won the oligarchy favour due to his handling of rural unrest and his opposition to Molina's modest land reforms. He appeared as the ideal man to maintain the status quo. For its part, the UNO presented the retired colonel Ernesto Claramount who received the support of reformist soldiers.

The months leading up to the elections exacerbated tensions but the situation flared up when the results of the polls were released. The PCN won the elections following a flagrant fraud in the vote count. In response, crowds estimated at 50,000, gathered in Plaza Libertad in central San Salvador. On the night of 28 February 1977, soldiers and police forces, supported by UR-416 tankettes, trucks equipped with high-pressure water lances and tear gas, intervened. According to the press at the time, there were five dead, 60 injured and 200 arrests.[56] For others, the massacre left 50 to 100 dead. The bodies were quickly evacuated, and the place cleaned of blood.[57] This event reinforced the growing belief that the oligarchy and the FAES would never cede power of their own free will. After the 'stolen' elections of 1972, those of 1977 convinced thousands of Salvadorans of the impossibility of peaceful political change.

Romero's presidency was taking place in troubled times. All traces of political openness made by Molina were cancelled and repression increased. The promulgation of the Law for the Defence and Guarantee of Public Order in November 1977 eliminated almost all legal restrictions on violence against civilians and put an end to any democratic façade in El Salvador. But the toughening of the legislation was far from calming the political climate. On the contrary, the escalation of violence was accelerating and deepening. Between July 1977 and October 1979, the state was responsible for the deaths of 461 people and the disappearance of 131.[58]

In addition to the security forces, the *Organización Democrática Nacionalista* (National Democratic Organisation or ORDEN), founded by Julio Rivera in 1966 in order to monitor the rural population and combat communist agitation, participated in this repression. From 1972, they extended their actions against the universities after President Molina ordered their occupation by the security forces, causing the death of many students and professors.[59] The repression hit well beyond what could be considered the Left. Thus, the PDC supporters became the target, which destroyed their ability to act as a legal and electoral opposition. This government attack on the Centre led to a radicalisation of the opposition, which benefited the far Left.

From 1976–1977 the occupations of public places increased, the Ministry of Labour in November 1977, the Cathedral of San Salvador and the embassies of Costa Rica, Panama, Venezuela and Switzerland in February 1978 with UN and OAS representations in June 1978 and the Mexican Embassy and the Red Cross offices in January 1979. Demonstrations were often accompanied by armed commandos. Thus, in May and October 1977, the demonstrators responded with arms to police repression. Although the government enacted a law at the end of 1977 which made it possible to drive out the peasants who had invaded the land, the occupations multiplied as well as the workers' strikes in the cities. Several erupted in March and April 1979 and that of an energy company managed to suspend the distribution of electricity at the national level.[60]

In this context, Jimmy Carter became President of the United States in Washington. Until then, the Americans had been the mentors of the Salvadoran FAES and agro-export sector, partly financing the economic and social development programme initiated by the military. The Nixon and Ford administrations also complacently turned a blind eye to the use of electoral fraud in 1972 and 1977. Carter decided to condition the payment of military aid to El Salvador on respect for human rights. In reaction, Romero decided to refuse it.[61]

Two years after the start of his presidential mandate, General Romero abandoned the reformist projects of his predecessors for a purely repressive policy. By early 1979, the country was on the brink of chaos and its government was cut off from almost all outside support. Romero was internationally accused of human rights violations whilst the UNO refused to participate in the 1978 elections.

Under the impetus of President Carter, Washington maintained its pressure on the Salvadoran government to reduce the level of violence. Romero made a few promises which failed to pacify the country. On the contrary, his retreat was frowned upon by the oligarchy and the hard core of the FAES, who withdrew their support whilst the promises of political reform were not believed, neither by the Left, nor by the United States. It was in this difficult situation that the fall of the Somoza regime in neighbouring Nicaragua accelerated the crisis.

The 1979 revolution in Nicaragua led many officers of the Somoza's troops to flee to El Salvador before joining other countries of exile. The spectacle of these defeated soldiers made Salvadoran officers fear that they would experience the same fate. The blows were therefore redoubled against the opposition. Between 1st May and 15 June 1979, the UGB committed 13 attacks. Professors and peasants suspected of sympathising with the opposition, were

BPR militants occupied the French and Venezuelan embassies, in front of which 14 supporters were killed by the National Guard on May 1979. (Albert Grandolini Collection)

murdered by the security forces whilst the offices of the opposition newspaper *La Cronica* were set on fire and a transmitter of Radio YSAX was destroyed.[62]

The Sandinistas' victory had the effect of galvanising Left-wing activists who believed that the emergence of a 'Salvadoran socialist society' was near since 'if Nicaragua has triumphed, El Salvador will triumph'.[63] The commotion redoubled. At the end of April, the BPR led the occupation of streets and factories by armed militants. The FPL were multiplying armed propaganda actions, building barricades on the roads, burning buses. Peasants were seizing land, workers were occupying factories to demand higher wages whilst slum dwellers demonstrated to demand land for building homes. The BPR, the FAPU and the PCS thus organised about 20 strikes in August and September 1979.[64]

On 9 May 1979, the GN opened fire on 100 demonstrators, killing 25 people and wounding 70 in front of foreign press correspondents. To protest against this new massacre, armed BPR militants seized the Cathedral of San Salvador and also the embassies of France, Costa Rica and Venezuela, whose staff were taken hostage. On 21 May, BPR demonstrators near the Venezuelan embassy were attacked by the police, killing 19 people. In retaliation, the FPL assassinated the Minister of Education on 23 May.[65] The next day, the government declared a state of siege. The FPL also executed Hugo Wey, a Swiss diplomat and then fired on the South African embassy.[66] The country was desperately approaching chaos. President Romero's inability to contain the violence, and even more, his permissiveness in the face of violence committed by the security forces, demanded a solution that could not wait.

Faced with the deterioration of the situation, reformist soldiers decided to act. Their goal was to install a government that would put an end to the actions of the death squads and allow an increase in the standard of living of the population by distributing the land fairly and restoring the failing economy. They first met with several influential civilians to convince them to have President Romero resign. Faced with the failure of this attempt, they decided to prepare a coup by recruiting young progressive officers. Meetings were held with Archbishop Romero, whose support should help legitimise the coup and win it the support of the masses.[67]

At the same time, pressure continued to mount on President Romero. The Carter administration ordered him to resign or bring forward the date of the presidential elections. Romero announced, at the beginning of August, the lifting of the state of siege, a 20 percent salary increase and the authorisation of exiles to return to El Salvador. A few days later, he finally declared the holding of early presidential elections. It was already too late for him. Reformist military officers consulted the US Embassy. Washington's official position on the Coup was one of neutrality.

The coup took place on the morning of 15 October 1979. After ensuring that the barracks were neutralised, Colonel Jaime Abdul Gutiérrez called Romero and the FAES high command. He informed them that the president was no longer in power and demanded that he and some officials of his regime left the country. Romero asked the GN for help, but some of these units were controlled by the plotters whilst the others remained passive. He and his cabinet then left the country after a bloodless coup.[68]

Washington quickly recognised the new government, the *Junta Revolucionaria de Gobierno* (Revolutionary Government Junta or JRG), restored economic and military aid and urged it to carry out reforms. The two main concerns of the United States were the repression of the guerrillas of El Salvador to prevent the country from knowing the fate of Nicaragua and the end of human rights violations. The installation of the JRG was therefore welcomed, despite the doubts that existed about its ability to overcome the resistance of Right-wing paramilitary groups.

2
1980 – THE YEAR OF SHATTERED HOPES

From the Coup of 1979, El Salvador entered a serious crisis, divided between three very different political projects. The conservative project, led by the forces that were ousted from power; the modernising reformist project, directed by the JRG and finally the revolutionary project of the Left-wing politico-military groups which would come together in the FMLN. The year 1980 chronicled the bankruptcy of the reformist project and of the JRG which embodied it. This failure opened the road to civil war.

Hopes and Disappointments of the JRG

On 15 October 1979, the progressive soldiers who dominated the JRG published a proclamation which constituted one of the most categorical denunciations of the inequalities within El Salvador. They pledged to end human rights violations and political violence, whilst announcing measures to achieve a fair distribution of national wealth, including land reform, nationalisation of banks and foreign trade.[1] To implement this programme, the JRG had in its ranks (alongside two soldiers), three civilians from the moderate opposition, whilst the government was made up of representatives of most of the political parties of the time, including the Left. Among the first measures taken, the JRG ordered the dissolution of ORDEN and increased the minimum wage for day labourers to stimulate the economy and demonstrate its support for the peasants. Nevertheless, the obstacles appeared quickly.

If the JRG disbanded the ORDEN, it received no cooperation from the local GN commanders, generally seen as controlling it. Nor could it prevent these commanders from continuing to serve the interests of the landowners using violence and intimidation.[2]

For their part, the projects of agrarian reform, nationalisation of banks and foreign trade were ambitious and clashed with the interests of the oligarchy. Thus, the agrarian reform, wanting to respond to the aspirations of many landless peasants and to the leaders of the Centre and the Left, was proving disappointing in its objectives. When the decree on its application was published in March 1980, the situation in certain rural areas was already one of open conflict where soldiers and guerrillas clashed. Above all, at this time, power was already firmly assured in the hands of soldiers determined to defend the privileges of the bourgeoisie.

Although the coup met with virtually no opposition from the FAES, only 20 percent of the officer corps supported the reforms. The majority seemed to belong neither to the reformist camp nor to the conservative camp. Although they shared a general feeling of anti-communism and a strong attachment to the military institution, they were not sufficiently convinced of the need for the type of radical reform advocated by the JRG which they only supported in order to prevent a revolution. Therefore, they opted for a kind of neutrality which ultimately worked in favour of the conservative faction. In this situation, the reformists were quickly defeated in the struggle for control of the FAES.[3]

The conservative military gradually imposed itself, as shown by the appointment of Colonel José Guillermo Garcia to the Ministry of Defence, of Colonel Nicolas Carranza as Deputy Minister, of Eugenio Vides Casanova as head of the GN and of Reynaldo Lopez Nuila at the direction of the PN. Colonel Gutiérrez, the most prominent member of this conservative faction, succeeded in reorganising the FAES under his control.[4]

The level of repression after the coup increased compared to that of the Romero regime. On 16 October 1979, due to strikes being illegal under the Public Order Act, 78 striking workers were arrested and 18 were killed by the military. The ERP for its part, launched 'insurrectional actions' in peripheral neighbourhoods of San Salvador. In San Marcos, Cuscatancingo and Mejicanos activists took to the streets, built barricades and called on people to join them. The security corps supported by armoured vehicles, attacked the barricades and after hours of fighting, the members of the ERP fled, not without having suffered heavy losses.[5] Amnesty International also reported that in the week following the coup, there were more than 100 killings of strikers occupying farms and factories. During the months of October and November, the streets were the scene of confrontation between the GN and the troops of the BPR and the FAPU. The JRG, unable to control this growing spiral of violence and faced with the rise of the conservative FAES faction, resigned in early 1980.

Faced with the growth of Left-wing armed groups, the security forces became more brutal and mercilessly tracked down opponents. (Albert Grandolini Collection)

On the day of Archbishop Romero's funeral, the security forces did not hesitate to fire on the crowd who had come to pay homage to the man who embodied opposition to the military regime. (Albert Grandolini Collection)

Quickly, a second JRG was formed based on an agreement between the PDC and the FAES, but without the presence of representatives of the Left. The PDC regained a central place in Salvadoran politics but it lost much of its popular support due to the defection of many of its members who preferred to join popular organisations. This weakened them against the conservatives of the FAES and the oligarchy. The entry of the PDC into the JRG was nevertheless, strongly supported by the United States and pressure from Washington should be allowed it to engage in economic reforms, put an end to repression and dialogue with popular organisations.

Despite American encouragement, the JRG found itself increasingly isolated to the Right, with only the support of the PDC and the traditional oligarchy. The murder by the security forces of 67 Left-wing activists during a demonstration in San Salvador on 22 January 1980, definitively cut off popular organisations whilst the far Right fuelled the climate of violence. The assassination of prosecutor Zamora, on 25 February 1980, was preceded by a speech on the radio by Major Roberto D'Aubuisson, head of the UGB, who denounced him as a member of the FPL.[6] The murder of Zamora, which symbolised the progressive military's failure to stop the violence, precipitated the fall of the second JRG on 3 March 1980.

The third JRG brought Duarte to the forefront of the political scene when he entered the Junta on 6 March. Duarte, a powerful figure in the PDC and enjoying strong support from the United States, brought back hope for a centrist solution to the country's problems. He was considered the only man capable of overcoming the intransigence of the Right and bringing the Left back into the political game. For this, the JRG undertook to implement land and banking reforms, but it also proclaimed a state of siege, which suspended all constitutional guarantees for 30 days and which would be extended for one year. This measure, instead of accelerating the implementation of reforms, was used by the FAES to block them.[7]

The violence escalated with the assassination of Archbishop Romero, shot dead by an unknown man whilst saying mass on 24 March 1980. Condemnation of the murder came from all over the world. A crowd estimated at over 80,000 gathered to mourn

From 1979, the PCS choose the path of armed struggle and set up a military structure, the FAL. This abandonment of legal political action allowed the rapprochement between the communists and the other armed organisations of the Left. (Albert Grandolini Collection)

Romero's death the day after his assassination. A shooting broke out which left between 23 and 30 dead and around 200 injured.[8] On the day of the Archbishop's funeral, a crowd of around 50,000 people gathered outside the Cathedral of San Salvador. Many bishops from various Latin American countries were also present. Before the start of the mass, the security forces fired on the crowd whilst urban guerrillas responded with gunfire. There were many dead and injured.[9] The PDC justified the massacre and definitively cut itself off from the Left.

Thus, little by little, to defeat the extreme Left, the JRG chose the military option rather than reforms. At the same time, the consolidation and unification of the Left was a reaction to failed reforms and increased repression by the military and death squads.

The Unification of the Left

Throughout the 1970s, the Salvadoran Left remained deeply divided. It was still so in the face of the October 1979 coup when certain organisations such as the RN, showed a certain neutrality towards the JRG whilst the ERP called for insurrection. In a few months, the situation was reversed. The reasons for the unity of the Left were the failure of the progressive military to push for reforms, the movement of the JRG to the Right and the increase in repression.

Within the PCS, the presidential elections of 1977 demonstrated that electoral struggle was useless and debates began on the need for armed struggle. In 1978, seven executives of the PCS were sent to Nicaragua to fight in the ranks of the Sandinistas.[10] For a long time, the rejection of the armed struggle by the PCS angered Castro, who withdrew his support and gave it to the FPL and then to the ERP. This changed with the 7th Congress in July 1979, when the PCS declared itself in favour of a violent revolution.[11] It appointed a Military Commission and accelerated the transformation of self-defence groups into popular militia, a new urban guerrilla structure whose task was to recover vehicles, steal or buy weapons. This eventually led to the creation of the *Fuerzas Armadas de Liberacion* (Liberation Armed Forces or FAL) on 24 March 1980.

The FAL, whose implementation was entrusted to José Luis Merino Hernandez alias Ramiro Vasquez, head of the Military Commission, quickly absorbed the militias and self-defence units. With few members but well organised, the FAL mainly recruited among the militants of the PCS and Communist Youth but also trade unionists, members of student or peasant organisations. At the beginning of 1980, a detachment of 50 militants went to Cuba to receive officer training. This allowed the FAL to develop urban and

Fidel Castro played a fundamental role in the creation of the FMLN. Without his authority, his power of persuasion and the help he could give them, it would have been almost impossible to unite the Salvadoran revolutionary organisations. (Author's Collection)

rural military formations in different areas of the country, including the Santa Ana and San Salvador departments and north of San Vicente department.[12]

The rallying of the PCS on the path of armed struggle removed the last obstacle between the communists and the other revolutionary formations and made it possible to accelerate their rapprochement. On 11 January 1980, the *Coordinadora Revolucionaria de Masas* (Revolutionary Coordination of the Masses or CRM) was formed, which brought together the BPR, the FAPU, the *Union Democratica Nacionalista* (Nationalist Democratic Union) and the LP-28. This structure had to coordinate the actions of the groups that were its members. On 22 January, it organised a large demonstration to commemorate the *Matanza* of 1932 which brought together more than 200,000 people who marched to the Cathedral Square in San Salvador. Security forces fired on peaceful protesters who were only defended by Left-wing military groups who practised armed self-defence. Salvadoran Human Rights Commission said the shooting killed 67 people whilst 250 were injured.[13] The violence of the military demonstrated once again that they would not tolerate any opposition from the Left.

The assassination of prosecutor Zamora accelerated the division of the PDC. In March, a Democratic Front brought together the moderate Left and former members of the PDC and the MNR leader Guillermo Manuel Ungo. This Democratic Front was closer to the Coordinadora Revolucionaria de Masas (Revolutionary Mass Coordination or CRM) and from their union in April, the *Frente Democrático Revolucionario* (Revolutionary Democratic Front or FDR) was born which would be a faithful ally to the guerrillas during most of the civil war.[14]

The FDR offered a unitary structure to groups, ranging from the moderate Centre to the extreme Left. Its stated aims include the establishment of a pluralistic government, respect for human rights, a mixed economy and non-alignment in foreign policy. The national stature of its main leaders, often former members of the JRG gave it a strong following whilst the moderation of its programme and the prestige of these leaders, allowed it to obtain international support. Above all, the birth of the FDR demonstrated a hitherto unknown solidarity within the opposition and the possibility of its unification.

Cuba played an important role in the unification of the El Salvador Left. After the turn of the PCS towards the armed struggle, the Cubans were committed to moving forward. Above all, Fidel Castro actively assumed the role of intermediary to unify the various revolutionary groups. On 17 December 1979, he brought together Cayetano Carpio for the FPL, Ernesto Jovel of the RN and Schafik Handal of the PCS, to form the *Coordinora Politico Militar* (Political Military Coordination or CPM) which was officially born on 9 January 1980.[15]

The process of unification was, nevertheless, difficult. In early 1980, the Cuban representative for El Salvador convened a meeting of guerrilla leaders in Managua. The Cubans and the Nicaraguans announced that they were ready to provide arms and military training to the Salvadorans on the condition that they united and formed a single opposition front, as the Sandinistas did.[16] Despite this pressure, on 1st April, when a CPM meeting was called to discuss the ERP's application for membership, Fermán Cienfuegos, RN representative, opposed it. He accused Villalobos and Ana Guadalupe Martinez of having repeatedly tried to assassinate him and other RN leaders. It was not until the last days of April that Cienfuegos finally accepted ERP membership.

At its birth, the FMLN was only a coordinating body of which each member organisation retained its own structures. The process of unification would be done gradually during the civil war. (Author's Collection)

In early May, discussions began to move from the coordination of revolutionary organisations to the creation of a single leadership. Again, Jovel, leader of the RN, publicly declared that he could not ally himself with the ERP which assassinated Roque Dalton. It took all of Castro's persuasion to get him to reverse his decision. This process concluded on 22 May when the leaders of the FPL, ERP, RN and PCS met in Havana to create the *Direccion Revolucionaria Unificada* (Unified Revolutionary Directorate or DRU).

The DRU, composed of 12 members, three representatives of each organisation, was quickly recognised by the

FDR as the military arm of the revolution. Its birth, however, brought only a precarious unity between ideologically disparate organisations. In September, the RN even announced its departure from this organisation. It was only the death of Jovel in a plane crash that led his successor, Fermán Cienfuegos, to agree to join the DRU. Above all, the Cuban threatened to stop supporting the Salvadoran guerrillas if it was disunited which was a decisive argument.[17]

The first decision of the DRU was the organisation of an international tour to solicit support from abroad. Schafik Handal was responsible for travelling to the socialist countries of Eastern Europe and as far as Vietnam. Another mission was assigned to Carpio and Domingo Santacruz who visited the presidents of Central America whilst Villalobos and Cienfuegos travelled to Panama and Mexico. Nevertheless, the DRU was not very operational and was undermined by divisions on which strategy to adopt with each organisation continuing to act independently.[18]

On 10 October 1980, Cuban efforts finally led to the creation of the FMLN which brought together the FPL, the RN, the ERP and the PCS before incorporating the PRTC in December. This birth did not however put an end to the divisions between the five organisations that made up the FMLN. Distrust remained great between the ERP and the RN whilst the latter were critical of the PCS, which considered them for its part, as 'petty-bourgeois adventurers'.

The first steps of this fragile unit of the Left were part of a climate of intensification of repression against the opposition. The third JRG had to face the rise of popular anger which resulted in a general strike on 24 and 25 June and then again from 13 to 15 August. The repression was more ferocious as illustrated by the Rio Sumpul massacre on 13 and 14 August where the *Destacamento Militar* (Military Detachment or DM) No.1 and the GN, killed around 300 people. On 27 November, in the afternoon, six FDR leaders were kidnapped on leaving the Externado de San José school and their mutilated bodies were found the next day. The murder, claimed by a death squad, managed to decapitate a non-clandestine popular organisation. On 2 December, at the Comalapa International Airport in San Salvador, four US nuns were kidnapped and murdered by GN agents. This event could not leave Washington indifferent.

The Salvadoran Crisis and the Cold War

In October 1979, when the JRG took power, the Carter administration was obsessed with the fear that the country would know the fate of Nicaragua. In November, faced with the weakness of the FAES and the security forces facing a conflict against guerrillas, it decided to send anti-riot equipment for US$200,000 as well as six instructors. It was hoped that the aid would ensure the JRG did not collapse but in exchange, Washington demanded the implementation of reforms and an alliance between the FAES and the PDC.

In February 1980, Carter announced he was exploring the possibility of economic aid amounting to US$50 million in loans to finance the reforms of the JRG and including US$5.7 million in military equipment. Washington also decided to send three military Mobile Training Teams (MTT) of 12 men each to El Salvador.[19] The United States still hoped for the implementation of reform, the end to repression and that the PDC and moderate political elements would be able to establish a link with the political Left before violence further radicalised it. Quite the opposite was happening, the massacres and violence were intensifying.

Despite the assassination of Archbishop Romero, Washington continued to support the JRG, supplying it with six UH-1H helicopters. In August 1980, it finally granted the credit of US$6 million for the purchase of transport, communication and riot control equipment.[20] Nevertheless, the murder of the six FDR leaders in November and the discovery of the bodies of the four American nuns on 4 December, led to the suspension of aid. In response to this decision, Duarte was appointed president of the JRG and Gutiérrez commander of the FAES in order to appease Washington. Finally, on 17 December, the United States agreed to provide US$20 million in economic aid to El Salvador, but no military aid.

The discovery of the bodies of four American nuns murdered by members of the GN demonstrated the brutality of the Salvadoran security forces and provoked the suspension of the US military aid. (Author's Collection)

On 3 January 1981, a death squad made up of GNs, assassinated José Rodolfo Vieira, President of the Institute in charge of the application of agrarian reform and two American civilians who were accompanying him, at the exit of the Sheraton Hotel in San Salvador.[21] Despite this further killing of American citizens, on 14 January, Carter resumed military aid after receiving information that the FMLN was growing stronger and now posed a serious threat to the JRG. The same day, the leaders of the Left expressed the wish to open negotiations with the United States for a political settlement of the conflict which was beginning. Washington refused and on 16 January, Carter approved an additional US$5 million in combat aid and another US$5 million four days later.[22] The Carter administration refused that notion that the domino theory could be applied in Central America whilst the victory of the Sandinistas in Nicaragua with the help of Cuba, transformed the region into one of the battlefields of the Cold War.

It was true that the seizure of power by the Sandinistas in Nicaragua in July 1979 accelerated the growth of the Salvadoran guerrilla apparatus. Salvadorans fought in the ranks of the Sandinistas against Somoza and it seemed obvious that Nicaragua could now serve as their rear base. Above all, it seemed that the Sandinista example could lead El Salvador down the same path. This perspective was heard in Moscow where, on 20 October 1980, the Soviet leader Boris Ponomarev declared that the Sandinista victory offered hope that Central American countries could 'be expected to undergo revolutionary changes of "a socialist transformation" '.[23] On 28 April 1980, in the Hungarian Embassy in Mexico City, the leaders of Left-wing armed groups met with representatives of East Germany, Bulgaria, Poland, Vietnam, Cuba and the USSR to ask

Shafik Handal, leader of the PCS, visited the countries of the Socialist Bloc and its allies during the summer of 1980 and managed to obtain the necessary weapons to equip the FMLN forces. (Author's Collection)

them for arms. In Cuba, they even met the leader of the GDR, Erich Honecker.[24]

In June–July, with the help of Soviet officials in charge of Third World affairs, such as Karen Brutens and his deputy Kudachkin, Schafik Handal visited the USSR and some Eastern European countries. Nevertheless, the Soviet leadership remained cautious, and Handal never met with senior officials or received any response to a request for help.[25] He then went to Vietnam to meet Le Duan, Secretary General of the Communist Party. Hanoi agreed to provide approximately 1,500 American-made M-16 and AR-15 rifles, 210 machine guns, 48 mortars, 12 RPG-2s and thousands of rounds of ammunition. From 19 to 24 June, Handal was in East Berlin where Honecker promised to provide equipment and military training. He then visited Prague and Sofia who offered weapons and equipment. In Budapest, the Hungarians promised to supply western weapons through Ethiopia and Angola. In Addis Ababa, President Mengistu Hailé Mariam agreed to provide 1,500 Thomson submachine guns, 1,500 M-1 carbines and 1,000 M-14 rifles. The Palestine Liberation Organisation (PLO) also promised in July to send arms to El Salvador whilst Iraq offered US$500,000.[26]

Handal succeeded in obtaining 130 tons of arms and materials, with the countries of Eastern Europe, except for Poland and Romania, agreeing to provide communication equipment, uniforms and medical products. The USSR only undertook to ensure the transport of this aid to Cuba and to train militarily, a dozen Salvadorans. Even if Moscow gave its support, it did not want, by providing substantial material aid, to appear too offensive in Central America and the Soviets denied sending any support to the FMLN.[27]

Cuba played a much more important role, first in the structuring of the guerrillas of El Salvador with the creation of the FMLN, but also as a logistician in the supply of weapons. For this, it used the shipping infrastructure set up to support the Sandinistas and which still existed after the sudden fall of Somoza.[28]

The interest of the Americans, the Soviets or the Cubans regarding the situation in El Salvador showed the failure of the political project of the JRG. The 1979 coup was the last hope of reaching a political agreement through the implementation of reforms in the political, economic and social fields. But the rise of violence generated by the Left and the Right, wasted the opportunity to avoid an armed conflict. For the Left, the triumph of the Sandinista revolution aroused the conviction that it was possible for it to seize political power through armed struggle. For its part, the alliance between the PDC and the FAES accentuated its orientation towards a counter-insurgency project to eliminate the Left. Once the FMLN became a truly unified military force, there was no other way out of the Salvadoran conflict but war.

3
FMLN FORCES VERSUS FAES

At its birth in late 1980, the FMLN was a disparate force. Each organisation had its own armed forces, distinct settlement areas and a preferred strategy. The task of unifying, or even simply coordinating, this diversity was the first mission of the FMLN. The second was to build a military force capable of confronting and defeating the FAES.

The Organisation of the FMLN

The FMLN was led by the DRU, which later took the name of *Comandancia General* (General Command or CG) and included the leaders of the five parties that composed it, Carpio for the FPL, Villalobos for the ERP, Jovel for the RN, Handal for the PCS and Roberto Roca for the PRTC.[1] Political leadership was assumed by the *Comisión Política* (Political Commission), made up of 15 members and the *Consejo Nacional* (National Council), a deliberative body, made up of 10 members per organisation. On the military level, the FMLN acquired a General Staff headed by Jorge Meléndez.[2]

The authority of the CG, based in Managua, was nevertheless, relative since each organisation retained its identity and its own structures. They therefore interpreted the directives of the CG freely in the territories they controlled. At first, the different groups were reluctant to cooperate with each other, a situation that gradually changed and allowed better cooperation towards the second half of the 1980s. However, they still maintained their separate command structures and their organic units throughout the conflict.

Whilst each organisation was equally represented within the CG, the ERP and the FPL were nevertheless, the most powerful. They had the most fighters and influence through the mass organisations. The latter served as the first lines of defence against the security services and base recruitment for the guerrillas. Mass organisations quickly lost their importance because all their important cadres were incorporated into the guerrilla forces which were being structured in the countryside.

Alongside the mass organisations, the FMLN could rely on the FDR. Although it was not directly part of the FMLN, the FDR, which was more of a social-democratic leaning, believed that the latter alone was capable of solving the problems affecting El Salvador. It played an important role in using the prestige and contacts of its leaders to gain international recognition for the FMLN from western countries, organise a global network of support and pressure the United States to reduce aid to the Salvadoran government.[3]

The Strategic Debate Within the FMLN

If the strategy of the FMLN was designed during the meetings of the CG, it gave rise to many intense debates. At the end of 1980, the FMLN looked for patterns in the recent past, particularly in that of the Vietnam War. The Salvadoran revolutionaries were indeed fascinated by Giap's theories on the revolutionary war which allowed the Vietnamese to defeat the United States, in particular by a strategy of attrition of their forces. Latin American revolutionary movements were also sources of inspiration, especially that of the Sandinistas, which demonstrated the viability of the revolutionary path to overthrow a weak and corrupt regime.[4]

These different models fed the strategic reflections of revolutionary groups and also contributed to the divisions that existed between them. The strategic analysis of the PCS was centred on insurrectional theory. It did not believe in the struggle of rural guerrillas as shown by the failures of Bolivia, Peru or Venezuela and favoured the creation of conditions for a popular insurrection. The ERP had a close position, believing that the population could overthrow a weak government if stimulated by spectacular military action. This type of popular participation appeared more essential to obtain a victory since it alone could suppress the military balance of power unfavourable to the revolutionaries.

The FPL positions were different. They considered the context of the Cold War to predict that Washington would not be able to accept that El Salvador could become a second Nicaragua. The American Armed Forces would therefore be obliged to intervene to prevent its fall. Under the conditions of an invasion of the country by US troops, the only possible strategy was that of prolonged resistance and guerrilla warfare from the Chalatenango and Morazan mountainous regions. If the war continued, the United States, as happened in Vietnam, would be forced to withdraw and the guerrillas could take power.

Joaquin Villalobos, the leader of the ERP, managed, with the support of the Cubans and the Nicaraguans, to impose his insurrectionary strategy on the whole of the FMLN. (Author's Collection)

At the end of 1980, the FMLN had around 2,000 to 3,000 full-time combatants, plus several thousand militiamen. (Author's Collection)

The FPL, therefore, set themselves the objective of establishing the infrastructure of the resistance in remote areas with the creation of guerrilla and militia units, the establishment of base camps and fortified areas, the organisation of villages to provide logistical support and recruits to the guerrillas. This strategy, championed by Carpio, the 'Ho Chi Minh of Latin America' fitted into the protracted people's war theory conceived by the Chinese and Vietnamese. It also received the support of the RN which saw the armed struggle as a gradual process.

In 1980, when these organisations united in the FMLN, these strategic differences did not disappear. With the recent victory of the Sandinistas, the Cubans insisted that the FMLN follow a similar strategy, which was to say the unleashing of a series of increasingly powerful urban insurgencies supported by the columns of guerrillas coming from the countryside, until the overthrow of the government. One of the arguments in favour of this strategy was to take advantage of the few weeks of existence of the Carter administration to seize power and confront the new, more conservative Reagan administration with a fait accompli.[5]

This model, imposed by the Cubans, corresponded to the strategy proposed by the ERP which took a dominant position within the FMLN. It was all the more necessary as Carpio, the leader of the

The FMLN had a significant proportion of women, estimated at 30 percent among the rank and file fighters. (Author's Collection)

FPL, believed that there was an opportunity to win quickly and bring down the government.[6]

The diversity of strategic conceptions existing within the FMLN was far from being a handicap. On the contrary, it allowed it to adapt its strategy to the circumstances it faced and not to lock itself into a rigid strategic scheme, as was the case with other Latin American guerrilla movements. To carry out its revolutionary project, the FMLN had to forge a military force based on each of the organisations that composed it.

FMLN Armed Forces

The PCS was the most recent member of the FMLN to have acquired military forces, the FAL. They began to make themselves known through small armed actions in the cities, such as the burning of buses in San Salvador and Santa Ana, carried out by the *Grupos de Accion Revolucionaria* (Revolutionary Action Groups or GARS); formed in 1976 by young communists who acted in teams of 3 to 5 activists.[7] These GARs were quickly dismantled by the security forces and the survivors joined the FAL. To supervise and direct these forces, a contingent of 20 to 30 militants of the PCS went to the USSR to receive accelerated military preparation. In addition to the links with the socialist countries, the FAL were also in contact with other communist military groups such as the officers of the Chilean Communist Party, refugees in Cuba, who participated in the preparation of the operational plans.

The FAL units grew throughout 1980 and established camps where militants could train and be equipped, mainly in the Usulatan, San Salvador and San Vicente department. They were then structured in squads, platoons and sometimes in columns of 80 to 120 men.[8]

In early 1979, the ERP was strong enough to launch a daring operation on 1 February, detonating bombs in the headquarters of the PN and GN in San Salvador and in that of the GN in San Miguel, resulting in 15 dead and 21 injured.[9] In the aftermath of the 15 October Coup, the ERP even organised an insurrection on the outskirts of San Salvador which proved to be a failure.

The military actions of the ERP, whose urban commandos comprised just over 200 members, multiplied in 1980. On 8 January, 30 fighters attacked the GN headquarters in San Salvador and fired for nearly 30 minutes at the building. On 3 March, two 106mm mortars fired the same building without however, doing any damage. On 25 March, the ERP simultaneously detonated 40 bombs

In 1980, FMLN fighters were poorly armed and inexperienced. To overcome this weakness, the guerrillas could count on the support of Cuba and Nicaragua. (Albert Grandolini Collection)

An FPL poster in the streets of San Salvador. The FAPL, the military organisation formed by the FPL was one of the most powerful of the FMLN and concentrated its forces in the Chalatenango department. (Albert Grandolini Collection)

throughout the country, 14 in San Salvador, four in Santa Tecla, 10 in Santa Ana, two in Ahuachapan, seven in San Miguel and three in Usulatan.

By the end of 1980, the ERP had experienced military cadres who had received training in various places. A group of militants fought with the Sandinistas in Nicaragua before returning to El Salvador. Other activists left for Lebanon thanks to Otelo Saravia Carvallo, a Portuguese soldier who took part in the military uprising of 25 April 1974 in his country. In Lebanon, they received military training given by the PLO. Other fighters voluntarily completed their military service in the FAES to learn how to handle arms. Close relations were established with Cuba. With these various supports, the ERP counted at the end of 1980, about a thousand full-time combatants.[10]

Like the other revolutionary organisations, it was at the end of 1978 that the FPL entered relations with the Sandinistas and the Cubans. This resulted in sending about 25 militants to Cuba, led by José Roberto Sibrian, who underwent military training before joining the Southern Front in Nicaragua where six were killed in combat. At the end of November 1979, an FPL delegation led by Carpio, went to Vietnam where it received military training, notably from Vo Nguyen Giap, before returning to El Salvador in April 1980. Another delegation went to Lebanon with the PLO.

Each organisation belonging to the FMLN had its own armed forces. This photograph shows armed MLP militants, the mass organisation linked to the PRTC. (Albert Grandolini Collection)

In El Salvador, the FPL practised urban guerrilla warfare. Thus, on 15 May 1979, they killed three PN agents who were watching the South African Embassy. On 20 September, 80 fighters attacked small GN posts in different towns. On 19 October, the FPL assassinated Colonel Simon Tadeo Martell.

In order to strengthen its military structures, which took the name of *Fuerzas Armadas Populares de Liberacion* (People's Armed Forces of Liberation or FAPL), the FPL transferred most of the cadres of mass organisations to them, managing to constitute platoons of 25 combatants who gathered in columns of 80 to 100 men. Their first actions took place in April 1980 with attacks on the small towns of Santa Rita and Potonico. At the end of 1980, the FPL had 1,200 combatants organised into 12 columns supported by 600 militiamen.[11]

In 1977, the leaders of the RN encountered the Sandinistas who put them in contact with the Cubans and particularly, with the President of Panama, Omar Torrijos. From 1977 to 1979, Torrijos would supply the RN with weapons by organising six clandestine flights. These left from Panama to Costa Rica where the weapons were unloaded and transported by land to El Salvador or by planes which landed on clandestine runways.[12] The RN established bases in Costa Rica where the fighters were trained by an Argentinian former Montoneros militant. In 1978 and 1979, the FARN developed and widened their fields of action. Under the direction of Eugenio Chicas Martinez, the urban commandos carried out sabotage operations, attacks against the security forces and kidnappings. In 1978, the RN carried out seven spectacular kidnappings of various Salvadoran and foreign businessmen for ransoms. During this time, the FARN military cadres received training in Nicaragua and in Cuba to direct the militiamen who were in the vicinity of San Salvador, the urban commandos and the units of the rural guerrillas.

Until 1978, the military structures of the PRTC were small and favoured self-defence organisations over urban commandos who had only 50 fighters in the San Salvador region and between 70 and 75 in the rest of the country. From April 1979, the PRTC changed strategy and developed the urban guerrilla commandos which, on 20 September 1979, kidnapped two American businessmen who were released against a ransom. In 1980, the PRTC military forces became the *Fuerzas Armadas Revolucionarias de la Liberacion Popular* (Revolutionary Armed Forces of Popular Liberation or FAR-LP). This was under the command of Jacinto Sanchez whose main establishment was north of San Vicente department, in the region of Guazapa, south of Usulatan and San Salvador departments. They set up a logistics base in Nicaragua with the help of the Sandinistas and launched their first major operation on 16 August 1980, by attacking the hamlet of Santa Rita in the San Vicente department.[13]

It was with these different groups that the FMLN sought to acquire a military force capable of confronting the FAES. Whilst some argue that the FMLN in 1980–1981 had 12,000 armed combatants, this figure appears to be exaggerated and the truth is closer to 3,500.[14]. According to the FMLN itself, the guerrillas had 2,800 equipped and trained fighters in 1980, a figure close to the estimates of the FAES intelligence services, which was 2,000.[15]

These forces were distributed geographically according to the areas of establishment of each organisation. From September 1980, the revolutionary forces organised the transition from urban guerrillas (which until then had been predominant) to rural guerrillas, by setting up different camps. Some of them failed like the RN in the municipality of Masahuat in the Santa Ana department which was dismantled and destroyed. It had more success in the Cerro de Guazapa, the Morazan, Usulutan, San Vicente and Cabañas departments.[16] The ERP established its strongholds in the eastern part of the country, in Morazan and the Jucuaran marshes, close to the border with Nicaragua, whilst the FPL dominated in Chalatenango. In order to unify and coordinate its forces locally, the FMLN set up a regional military organisation by dividing the country into four Fronts; the Central Front *'Modesto Ramirez'* in the San Salvador, La Libertad, Cabañas and Chalatenango departments; the Paracentral Front *'Anastasio Aquino'* in La Paz, San Vicente and Cuscatlan departments; the Eastern Front *'Francisco Sanchez'* in San Miguel, Usulutan, La Union and Morazan departments; the

This photo of FMLN fighters in Cerro de Guazapa on late 1980 illustrated their weakness at that time. They all wear civilian clothes and the weapons they wield were derisory in the face of the FAES. (Albert Grandolini Collection)

Western Front '*Feliciano Ama*' in Ahuachapan, Santa Ana and Sonsonata departments. In 1985, the Northern Front '*Apolinario Serrano*' also appeared in Chalatenango department.[17]

At the beginning of 1981, the FMLN forces were far from resembling a real army. The General Staff and the CG were in fact, more political than military bodies, whilst the lack of the means of communication between Managua and the forces in El Salvador and even between the latter, was another handicap. Additionally, another problem was the heterogeneity of the troops available, mixing guerrilla units, militias and urban commandos.[18]

The ransoms collected for the release of businessmen or official personalities allowed guerrilla organisations to finance the purchase of weapons. Here, the release of the Labour Minister on 6 November 1979. (Albert Grandolini Collection)

To improve the military capabilities of the FMLN, Cuba agreed to organise a training programme for about a thousand combatants whilst several hundred others were trained in Nicaragua. In Cuba, the trainings took place in the camp called Punto Cero. In Nicaragua, the training of Salvadorans took place underground to avoid detection by locals or foreigners. The logistical difficulties of sending militants abroad and returning them to their country meant that fewer guerrillas than the FMLN wished would receive military training and a significant number could not return before the outbreak of fighting.[19] The support of its foreign allies was also crucial for the arming of the FMLN.

The Weapon Supplies

During the 1970s, the various Left-wing armed organisations procured weapons by their own means. Roberto Cañas tells:

> The typical guerrilla fighter who joined an armed struggle during the early 1970s began to [conduct operations in which he could] capture weapons. So, night watchmen would come – we call them serenos here. We would make sure that they had weapons, and we would carry out an operation – to capture the gun[s]. There were also pawnshops … they sell weapons. This is because in El Salvador, in the country, people buy weapons. We began to familiarise ourselves with the weapons, to conduct an armed propaganda – a Vietnamese concept of [armed] struggle. But the guerrillas in El Salvador began to carry out kidnappings and there were deaths within the most distinguished families of this country. Because the first money that financed the armed struggle in this country was money received through kidnappings. In the organisation that I was involved in, we eventually accumulated $35 million. In order to carry out a struggle, you have to have funds. There was a lot of money here, a result of the fact that we were specialists when it came to kidnapping and robbing banks.[20]

At the end of 1980, the FMLN had significant and modern armament, here Belgian FAL rifles belonging to the FPL. (Albert Grandolini Collection)

The total amount of these ransoms was estimated at around US$50 million.[21] Activists travelled to Spain, Algeria, Belgium, the Netherlands, Honduras, Panama and Mexico to stock up on weapons. Purchases also took place in El Salvador where members of the PN and FAES soldiers sold arms and ammunition to the guerrillas. The RN sourced its supplies on the black market in North America and Panama, where it bought M-16 automatic rifles. Subsequently, a delegation was sent to Algeria and Lebanon to receive support. In Beirut, it met Yasser Arafat who undertook to send 30 tons of equipment including RPGs.[22]

The supply of weapons took on greater importance after the international tour of Handal in the socialist countries. In October 1980, these countries sent 120 tons of materials to Nicaragua and 300 to 400 tons to Cuba out of the 800 tons promised. To introduce this material in El Salvador, the FMLN developed the 'Plan Puente'. The armament, transported by the Soviets to Cuba, took the direction of Venezuela and Panama, to then reach Costa Rica or Nicaragua.[23] Air routes were used to join various improvised air tracks in El Salvador, mainly in areas controlled by the FPL. The amount of material to be transferred often required daily flights. The planes left from an isolated and hidden runway at Papalonal about 40km north of Managua and also from Costa Rica with the agreement of President Torrijos.[24]

These missions were dangerous as in addition to the dangers of the weather and the topography, it was a question of landing on makeshift tracks at the mercy of an intervention by the Salvadoran security forces or the FAES. Thus, on 15 June 1980, a Panamanian Aerocommander 560-1 had to make an emergency landing in San Miguel. It carried 22,000 7.62 calibre rounds for G-3 and FAL rifles. The airlift between Nicaragua and El Salvador was nevertheless suspended in September 1980 in the face of US protests, but resumed in October and became more and more intense, even using Cessnas and C-47s of the Sandinista Air Force.

On 24 January 1981, the Cubans decided on a large delivery of weapons on 24 January 1981 to the Hacienda La Sabana airstrip in the coastal area of the Zacatecoluca department. The operation was a failure. A twin-engine Cessna 310 with 55 FAL, M-16 rifles and thousands of cartridges, crashed. The Sandinistas took off in a Piper Aztec piloted by Juan Talavera, a Costa Rica citizen, which managed to land without damage in La Sabana. He had to wait for the transfer of the injured pilots, but his plane was spotted by a FAS C-47. The FAS sent 22 paratroopers, joined by 16 CIIFA trucks and a helicopter which brought other paratroopers. The FPL fighters decided to retreat but 28 were killed. One of the pilots of the first plane was also killed whilst the other died of his injuries. Talavera was taken prisoner.[25]

A sea route existed between Chinandega in Nicaragua and the coasts of Jucuaran in El Salvador. In June 1980, the ERP set up a team in Jucuaran responsible for organising the transport of weapons by sea, under the direction of Remberto Centeno. Between October and the end of December, three maritime convoys brought 28 tons of equipment. On 25 January 1981, a last trip arrived at El Zompopero beach, south-east of the Conchagua volcano.[26]

Land arms supply routes were also organised which left from Nicaragua, sometimes from Costa Rica to cross Honduras and Guatemala.[27] The weapons travelled in trucks with double bottoms or fitted caches. At the beginning of 1981, the Hondurans intercepted a convoy of trucks coming from Nicaragua. It contained 100 M-16 and AR-15 automatic rifles, 50 81mm mortar grenades and thousands of rounds. Weapons warehouses were also discovered in Honduras, Costa Rica and Guatemala. Thanks to the overland route, at the end of 1980, the clandestine depots of the ERP in the San Salvador region received two to three containers each week, each containing 100 to 200 rifles. According to the FMLN, between 200 and 400 tons of materials managed to enter El Salvador to equip the guerrillas. The figure put forward by Colonel Gutiérrez, a member of the JRG, was 600 tons.

The FMLN also set up clandestine arms manufacturing workshops on Salvadoran territory. On 27 January 1980, the FAES discovered one of these workshops, belonging to the FPL near Ahuachapan, capable of producing tubes for mortars, anti-personnel mines, hand bombs, rocket launchers.[28] It was with these weapons that the guerrillas had to face the FAES.

The PRTC recruited largely from the ranks of the MLP to create its armed forces, the FAR-LP on 1980. (Albert Grandolini Collection)

For many young people from the middle class, like these young cadets who joined the Military Academy in 1983, becoming an officer represented an opportunity to rise socially. (Albert Grandolini Collection)

FAES Soldiers received mortar training. (Albert Grandolini Collection)

The Panhard AML was a light armoured car. Light, fast, agile and powerfully armed with a 90mm cannon and an AA 52 machine gun, it was designed for counter-insurgency operations during the Algerian war. (Albert Grandolini Collection)

The organisation of the FAES was based on conscription and one year military service for each male citizen aged 18 to 30. Before 1981, conscription was little used and most recruits were young poor peasants attracted by pay. Once this year was over, the conscripts joined the active reserve and had to attend training at the weekend in the barracks closest to their home. From the age of 30, those who were volunteers could go to the Territorial Service present throughout the country whilst others were integrated into the ORDEN.[29]

At the beginning of 1981, the FAES had 9,850 soldiers, including 9,000 in the Army, 100 in the National Navy and 750 in the FAS.[30] Russel Crandall gives higher numbers, between 13,000 to 20,000 people.[31] The army was therefore the most important component of the FAES with five Infantry Brigades which were little more than reinforced battalions, one Light Infantry Battalion, seven Independent Infantry companies called Military Detachments, three companies of Commandos and two companies of Paratroopers. Each Infantry Brigade was organised into one Battalion of 740 men comprising three Rifle Companies of 160 men each, one Command and Service Company and one Heavy Weapons Company.

The soldiers were armed with G-3 A3 rifles which could also launch M60P1 anti-personnel grenades and M60 AT anti-tank grenades whilst the officers were armed with HP Browning pistols and Uzi and HK MP-5 submachine guns. Each infantry squad had Browning machine guns and the infantry sections had HK-21 machine guns. The companies also had Stokes-Brandt M1 and M19 60mm mortars, M18 57mm recoilless rifles and 89mm rocket launchers. The FAES also used Browning M1919/A6 machine guns.

For its artillery, the Army bought from Yugoslavia in the early 1970s, four Zastava M-56 105mm batteries, three M52A2 AA 20mm batteries, 60 UBM-52 120mm heavy mortars. Thus in 1980, they had three artillery battalions equipped with M-101A1, M-56

The FAES in Crisis

In 1824, President Manuel José Arce founded the Salvadoran Army. Advised by French soldiers, it became a disciplined force with infantry, cavalry and artillery units. At the beginning of the twentieth century, the FAES became more professional by adopting the Prussian military model and El Salvador acquired one of the largest Armed Forces in Central America. Nevertheless, if the military dominated the political life and if the FAES emerged victorious from the war against Honduras in 1969, they experienced a deep crisis during the 1970s.

and AA M55A2. In addition, there was a Battalion equipped with 75mm M-116s.

The Army also included a Cavalry Regiment which had 12 AML-90 armoured cars and 10 UR-416 APCs. The infantry units were supported by different vehicles, which were in fact, modified and armoured civilian vehicles called Astroboy or Mazinger, a solution found by the FAES to circumvent the embargo on arms sales in El Salvador after the 1969 war. Thus, the FAES had 23 M-114 Astroboy armoured personnel carriers (APCs), 14 Mazinger, as well as a dozen armoured vehicles of various other types.[32]

Since 1959, the FAES ground forces had been able to rely on the Territorial Service, made up of volunteer reservists. This had the dual mission of providing immediate reinforcements to FAES units and helping the State with social and territorial control, joining forces in this last task with other organisations such as ORDEN and the *Agencia Nacional de Seguridad Salvadoreña* (National Security Agency of El Salvador or ANSESAL). Between 1977 and 1979, the ORDEN, which depended directly on the President of the Republic, would have had between 50,000 and 100,000 members, but its real core would not had exceeded 10,000 focused on rural intelligence. At the end of 1979 it was officially dissolved, and it was quickly replaced by the Civil Defence organisations proposed by the United States.[33]

The Navy, whose main base was in La Union, in 1981 had six American-built ships used for modest coastguard missions: two Mk IV type ships, a Stewart patrol boat and three Camcraft patrol boats. It brought together about 200 men, including 40 sailors who had training as infantrymen and were responsible for protecting the installations.[34]

Salvadoran Air Force

Origins of the *Fuerza Aérea Salvadoreña* (FAS, Air Force of El Salvador) can be traced back to 1917, when the Mexican government donated two TNCA Series A aircraft. The *Flotilla Aérea Salavdorena* was officially established on 20 March 1923 and received its first aircraft a year later – in form of five Italian-made SAML Aviatik bomber-reconnaissance biplanes – by which time a Flying Training School had been established at Ilopango, which became the main base. Despite the turmoil of the 1940s, the Salvadoran government acquired a number of training aircraft from US war surplus stocks, including Fairchild PT-19s and Boeing-Stearman PT-13A Kaydets, Vultee BT-13 basic trainers and Beech AT-11 Kansan twin-engined light bombers, of which the latter were also deployed as light transports and communication aircraft. El Salvador's participation in the Rio Pact of Mutual Defence in 1947 resulted in the arrival of a Military Mission from the USA, which completely reorganised and re-equipped the air force, and helped create the Engineering School. By the 1960s, the FAS thus operated a number of North American T-6 trainers and Douglas C-47 Skytrain transports, followed by the acquisition of three Beech T-34 Mentor primary trainers.[35]

Although the air force remained relatively small and was considered one of 'quartels' – or divisions – in the country's military hierarchy, the FAS experienced its most intensive period of growth during the 1960s, by when it was organised into three squadrons and had some 34 pilots. One of the units operated a mix of Cavalier P-51D Mustangs and Goodyear FG-1D Corsairs; another, Douglas B-26B Invaders, and the third, C-47s, including one each Beech AT-11 Kansan and Canadair DC-4M.

Whilst widely regarded as only 'fairly' trained, the service actually consisted of experienced and dedicated personnel, with good knowledge of their aircraft and the local terrain and it possessed a well-organised and trained Air Force Reserve, consisting of about 20 civilian pilots. However, the FAS had no autonomy and ran no joint exercises with the FAES and any movement of its aircraft and personnel was heavily curtailed by the Ministry of Defence. During the conflict with Honduras, the air force suffered significant combat losses, including two of its FG-1Ds and one Mustang, replaced by a rapid acquisition of at least 11 North American F-51D Mustangs and two Douglas B-26 Invaders (serials 600 and 601) from private sources in the USA.

However, efforts to acquire surplus North American F-86K Sabres jet fighters from Germany proved fruitless. Instead, El Salvador only managed to purchase four additional Invaders from Guatemala (serials 602, 603, 604 and 605). Although tensions with Honduras remained high, forcing the FAS to keep its fleet of vintage US-made aircraft operational, Invaders were in soon in such a poor shape that only three were nominally operational by 1972, when they were sold off, together with most of surviving F-51s and FG-1Ds.

Marred by an arms embargo imposed by the USA, and widespread corruption within the government, a new effort to rebuild the FAS

The MD.450 Ouragan was a fighter and ground attack aircraft, produced from 1951 to 1954 by the aircraft manufacturer Dassault. In 1974, 18 Israeli Ouragans were sold to El Salvador, where they ended their career in 1985. (Albert Grandolini Collection

Nine former Israeli and three French Fouga CM.170 Magisters were acquired by the FAS and used as both trainers and ground attack aircraft in the Salvadoran Civil War using bombs and nose-mounted 7.62mm machine guns. (Albert Grandolini Collection)

was initiated in 1973, when El Salvador purchased a total of 28 aircraft from Israel, including 20 Dassault MD.450 Ouragan jet-powered fighter-bombers, four Israel Aircraft Industries (IAI) Arava 201 short take-off and landing light transports, and four Fouga CM.170 Magister jet trainers.[36]

The first three Magisters (serials 500, 503, and 505) arrived per ship on 10 February 1974: the fourth (serial 507) followed in 1975. In 1978, three additional Magisters from surplus stocks of the French Air Force were acquired (serials 509, 510, and 511), powered by more powerful Marbore VI engines, but lacking internal armament.

Meanwhile, the first nine Ouragans (serials 700 to 708) reached El Salvador between May and August 1974 and were used to form the *Escuadrón de Caza y Bombardeo* (Fighter and Bomber Flight). Another 11 followed in 1975, but two of these never flew and were used as sources of spares only. Ouragans were old (manufactured in the second half of the 1950s) and slow but they were armed with four highly-effective DEFA cannon calibre 20mm and could carry a wide variety of unguided rockets and free-fall bombs, as well as Israeli-made napalm tanks. Moreover, one – serial 712 – was modified to carry the Israeli-made Shafrir Mk II guided air-to-air missiles. Perhaps unsurprisingly, the fleet experienced a relatively high attrition rate early on: one of the flyable examples (708) crashed on 18 August 1976 in the San Vicente area, another (710) on 15 June 1978 in the La Paz area, and the third (715) on take-off from Ilopango, on 23 April 1979.

Such and similar acquisitions of small numbers of aircraft and helicopters – including six SOCATA Rallye trainers and several helicopters from France of the mid-1970s – and FAS' never-ending efforts to overhaul and retain in service some of older types, created quite some confusion between foreign observers, resulting in very different reporting about the composition and equipment of the air force for the period 1979–1981.[37] With hindsight, it is certain that as of the time, the air force operated 15 Ouragans organised into the Fighter-Bomber Flight; six C-47s and four Aravas were operated by the *Escuadrón de Transporte* (Transport Flight), whilst the miscellany of Aérospatiale SA.315B Lama, Aérospatiale SE.316B Alouette III, Fairchild Hiller FH-1100, and Hughes/McDonnell MD.500D helicopters was operated by the Escuadrón de Helicópteros (Helicopter Flight). All

Geographical Distribution of FAES

Military regions	Military units	Location
San Salvador	1st Infantry Brigade	San Salvador
	FAS	San Salvador
	Artillery Brigade	Santa Tecla
	Cavalry Regiment	Santa Tecla
	Military Detachment No. 5 or DM-5	Cojutepeque
Santa Ana	2nd Infantry Brigade	Santa Ana
	DM-6	Sonsonate
	DM-7	Ahuachapan
San Miguel	3rd Infantry Brigade	San Miguel
	DM-3	La Union
	DM-4	San Francisco Gotera
	CICFA (Armed Forces Commando Training Centre)	San Francisco Gotera
El Paraiso	4th Infantry Brigade (created in 1980)	El Paraiso (Chalatenango Department)
	DM-1	Chalatenango
San Vicente	5th Infantry Brigade (created in 1981)	San Vicente
	DM-2	Sensuntepeque
	DM-IFA	Zacatecoluca
	CIIFA (Engineers Instruction Centre)	La Paz
Usulutan	6h Infantry Brigade	Usulutan

were home-based at Ilopango, but the FAS Meanwhile constructed another air base outside Las Flores, south of San Luis Taipa in the La Paz province and maintained around 30 airstrips elsewhere around the country.

A Politicised Officer Corps

Beyond this description of its organisation and its equipment, what characterised the FAES at the beginning of 1980 was the insufficiency of its armament which for a large part, was obsolete. Added to this problem were the structural weaknesses of the FAES management.

A GN patrol in a village in Northern El Salvador. (Albert Grandolini Collection)

Like in the rest of Latin America, the military career attracted young people from underprivileged classes because it allowed ordinary soldiers to have a salary and better living conditions. For officers, often from the middle classes, it allowed them to study and offered the opportunity to increase their social status, especially since each promotion from the Military Academy constituted a *tanda* whose members were commissioned and promoted together to each higher rank.[38] The idea was to encourage cohesion within the officer corps but with this system, Salvadoran officers were assigned to their posts based on seniority and political trustworthiness with their superiors, generally lacking dedication and basic military competence.

This conservatism of the officer corps pushed the FAES High Command to prepare throughout the 1970s for a new conventional war, like that of 1969 and to neglect the possibility of facing guerrillas – convinced that this type of combat was impossible due to unfavourable geographical conditions. For the military, the urban guerrilla warfare that predominated at the time was a matter of public order that fell exclusively to the security forces, neglecting to prepare for a counter-insurgency war. Another problem of FAES was the low presence of NCOs who, moreover, were not promoted according to their knowledge or experience in leadership.[39]

To this weaknesses were added the divisions born of the October 1979 Coup. About 50 senior officers were then dismissed which destabilised the high command. Tensions within the FAES, between the reformists represented by Colonel Majano and the conservatives, led by Colonel Gutiérrez and Colonel Garcia, were becoming increasingly strong. In January 1980, Colonel Majano was defeated and replaced in mid-May from his position as JRG commander whilst the officers who supported him, were transferred to lower positions. He was permanently expelled from the JRG in December 1980, then exiled, thus sealing the total control of the hardliners over the JRG and the FAES.[40]

It was in a weak position that the FAES began the civil war. Its equipment, its officers and its soldiers, as well as its strategy were totally unsuited to face a guerrilla war.

Security Forces

Alongside the FAES, El Salvador had security forces that depended entirely on the Ministry of Defence. The Directors of these security bodies were trusted by the President who therefore had significant powers and acted autonomously, even independently. In 1980 hey included 3,000 men divided between the GN with 1,000 members, the PN with 2,500 and the *Policia de Hacienda* (Treasury Police or PH) with 500. In 1988, their numbers increased to reach 4,200 for the GN, 6,000 for the PN and 2,400 for PH.[41]

Although the PH was originally responsible for fighting against propaganda at the borders, in 1980 it was largely involved in the fight against Left-wing guerrillas where it distinguished itself by violations of human rights. (Albert Grandolini Collection)

The GN, whose workforce was spread throughout the territory, was the largest and most effective security corps, especially in the fight against the Left in rural areas. Led by military officers, it had police and law enforcement missions in cities and in the countryside. The PN's mission was to fight crime in cities as well

The spectacle of people murdered by death squads and their bodies abandoned on the side of the roads to sow terror, became a daily occurrence in the late 1970s. (Albert Grandolini Collection)

as the surveillance of political opponents. This last activity was also entrusted to a specialised service, the Special Investigation Unit. The PH was responsible for combating smuggling at the borders, in ports and airports.[42]

These security corps were paramilitary organisations that wore military uniforms and whose main mission was to maintain order. During the 1970s, most of the fight against Leftist formations fell to them. In the cities, the PN, faced with demonstrations from the Left, used riot control units which were reinforced by the 4th Motorised Company equipped with Plymouth Volare vehicles. From 1979, these security forces nevertheless appeared insufficient in the face of the development of urban guerrilla warfare. They lacked special forces; the PN only had a Reaction Company, the GN a Direct Action Group and the PH, a company responsible for protecting foreign embassies. In order to keep the initiative, the PN formed the Special Anti-Terrorist Operations Section with 80 military reservists.[43]

Death Squads

Death squads did not belong to the security forces and were not state-owned or state-dependent organisations. Often born of private initiatives from Right-wing circles, they were nevertheless linked to the FAES and the security forces when they were not directly from them. According to the Truth Commission report, death squads:

> … consisted of organisations comprising groups of people who were usually dressed as civilians, were heavily armed, acted secretly, hid their association with the death squad and concealed their identity. They kidnapped members of the civilian population and rebel groups. They tortured hostages, concealed their whereabouts, and usually executed them … The squadrons, who were tied to state organisms through the latter's active collaboration or silent acquiescence, achieved a level of power that transcended that of an isolated or marginal phenomenon and became an instrument of terror and of the systematic physical elimination of political opponents. During the 1980s, many civilian and military authorities participated in, promoted and tolerated the actions of these groups.[44]

The death squads experienced a first development under the presidency of Romero. It was within the ORDEN that the members of the *Mano Blanca* (White Hand) were recruited while Major D'Aubuisson helped in the formation of the UGB in 1977, a squadron which had relations with the G-2, the GN intelligence service. In FAES units, S-II intelligence services also formed and used death squads whose operations were carried out by military personnel[45].

After a hiatus, following the October 1979 Coup, the death squads acted again in 1980 on a larger scale. According to some authors, in the early 1980s, they brought together around 6,000 people and 80,000 informants.[46] Until 1983, they attacked 15 to 18 victims a day, sometimes up to 30.[47]

On the national and international scene, D'Aubuisson was the most famous personality linked to the death squads. In 1979, he left the management of ANSESAL and made the link between civil and military groups, bringing the financial support of large landowners settled in Miami. He also established links with international anti-communist networks, notably in Guatemala, while the death squads benefited from the support of the Argentine dictatorship.[48]

Although much of the murders committed by the death squads were relatively indiscriminate and directed against people who fitted the profile of Left-wing sympathisers or who were peripherally involved in the opposition movement, they also dealt severe blows to the FMLN. Villalobos, head of the ERP, stated that between 1981 and 1983, the FMLN lost most of its urban network due to the actions of the death squads.[49]

US Military Aid

After Castro took power in Cuba in 1959, Washington was determined to avoid the establishment of 'another Cuba' in the western hemisphere that would not only threaten the Panama Canal but also jeopardise American national security. Keeping Latin America stable and orderly was also necessary to allow the United States to focus on other parts of the world. The communist threat was then used to justify the militarisation of the region and support for Right-wing dictators. It was within this framework that, since

It was under the impetus of the Kennedy Administration that Mobile Training Teams were sent to El Salvador to train the FAES. (Albert Grandolini Collection

Kennedy's presidency, the United States provided economic and military aid to El Salvador, even if it remained minimal.

The Pentagon provided this assistance in several ways. Among the most important were the Military Assistance Programme, the International Military and Education Training programme and the Foreign Military Sales programme. Another frequently used resource was the dispatch of MTTs often made up of special forces soldiers. Thus, from 1962 to 1965, 11 MTT of the 8th Special Force Group were in El Salvador to provide formation in different fields. As part of these programmes, many Salvadoran officers received training in US counter-insurgency doctrine at the American School of the Americas, created under Kennedy. These courses were originally held in the Panama Canal Zone but later moved to Fort Benning, Georgia.[50]

For its part, the Office of Public Safety, an aid programme for Latin American police forces, spent from 1957 to 1974, US$2.1 million for the formation of Salvadoran security forces, the supply of weapons, communications equipment and armoured vehicles. Between 1961 and 1977, about 300 members of the security corps received training in the United States, Panama and Puerto Rico whilst a team of five American advisors worked at the PN central garrison.[51] US Green Berets also advised and trained ORDEN leaders whilst other US servicemen provided technical assistance to ANSESAL as well as intelligence.[52]

Barely a month after the October 1979 Coup, on 13 November, the first military advisors of the US Military Advisory Group (Milgroup) arrived in El Salvador. They were led by Colonel Eldon Cummings. The latter was aware that the FAES had to modernise in order to face a guerrilla force stimulated by the Sandinista victory. Therefore, he asked that the G-3 rifles be replaced by modern M-16s to create commando units trained by Rangers or Airborne and to receive UH-1H helicopters. This advice was listened to and after the vote on 31 March 1980 by the American Congress for a programme of US$5.7 million of non-lethal equipment in El Salvador, the FAES requested the sending of six helicopters and the training of 20 pilots. Nevertheless, the new suspension of American aid at the end of 1980 postponed the date of delivery of the helicopters. It resumed at the beginning of January 1981, with the arrival on 7 January of 17 American military advisors from the Special Forces.[53] Washington's involvement in the Salvadoran conflict would continue to grow.

From Operation Rayovac to Operation Guazapa I, October 1980 – January 1981

If for years, the fight against Left-wing armed groups was the exclusive responsibility of the security forces, this situation was changing little by little, as the military actions of the revolutionaries took on a greater scale. From 1977, the FAES began to support the security forces in population control operations. In May 1980, the FAS supported ground troops in an operation north of Chalatenango department.[54]

The FAES were called upon again in October 1980 to intervene in the north of the Morazan department. This area, from the Torola River to the border with Honduras, was where the ERP and RN guerrilla camps were located and already had around a thousand combatants. In early October, the FAES planned a large scale operation, called Rayovac, to destroy these concentrations and mobilised around 2,500 soldiers.

From 1977, the FAES intervened more and more in the fight against Left-wing organisations. In this picture, soldiers arrest a young man who does not have identity documents. (Albert Grandolini Collection)

The Alouette III was a French multipurpose light helicopter which was widely used in operations against the FMLN at the beginning of the war. (Albert Grandolini Collection)

The soldiers encountered strong resistance on 4 and 5 October, in Cerro (Hill) Cacalote, which was at a height that allowed for good defence. The FAS had to step in to provide air support before the 105mm artillery guns came into action. The guerrillas eventually withdrew whilst the FAES forces continued to advance and reached Cerro El Mirador and then occupied Villa Rosario on 7 October. In the San Fernando area, the paratroopers managed to surround 150 guerrilla fighters after heavy fighting but the latter managed to flee before counter-attacking. The soldiers had to use machine guns, mortars and two Alouette helicopters to push them back.

After 11 days of fighting, the guerrillas tried to withdraw east of Jocoaitique and into the Meanguera area. Approximately 300 succeeded whilst 700 remained surrounded by the military. The latter bombarded with 105mm guns, the area of La Guacamaya where some of the rebels who fled the encirclement took refuge. The Commandos were ordered to advance on this sector. For two days, they confronted the rear guards of the guerrillas, reached La Guacamaya and continued to Arambala and the east of Perquin to search the area.

The company of the DM-4 which was in Sociedad, received the order to join San Fernando Gotera to carry out patrols in the north of this city until Torola River. Before crossing the river, the soldiers fell into an ambush but nevertheless managed to reach Meanguera.[55] During this operation on 13 October, the FAES committed the first of many massacres in the region, killing nearly a dozen unarmed civilians in La Guacamaya. Nearly a thousand non-combatants crossed the Honduran border to Colomancagua, which would become a UN refugee camp the following year.[56]

About two weeks after the end of Operation Rayovac, the FMLN returned to northern Morazan. Faced with this situation, the military decided to launch a new operation. About 600 Commandos and paratroopers supported by an artillery battery, combed an area from east to west from Corinto, passing through Joateca, Arambala, Perquin and up to San Fernando. However, the guerrillas –aware of the operation which was being prepared – evacuated the sector. Whilst the military advanced without encountering much resistance, the FMLN launched diversionary actions. Thus, about 100 combatants attacked the small garrison of Corinto from the surroundings of Joateca.[57]

In the early days of 1981, the FAES carried out other large scale military operations in both urban and rural areas in the San Miguel, La Union, San Vicente and Sonsonate departments and intensified their patrols throughout the country. On 4 January, an operation targeted the FMLN camps set up on the slopes of the San Salvador volcano. A few days later, the FAES attacked the Cerro de Guazapa where the first guerrilla camps had been set up at the end of 1978.[58]

This area, 35km north of San Salvador, was a strategic position that directly threatened the capital. North of the Cerro were also the sugar complexes of San Francisco and La Cabaña. The objective of Operation Guazapa I was to seize by surprise, the highest point of the Cerro – called El Roblar – and mobilised units of the 1st Infantry Brigade, security forces, FAS paratroopers, a squadron of the Cavalry Regiment, as well as batteries of 105mm howitzers and 81mm mortars, capable of striking guerrilla positions.

In the morning of 5 January, 50 paratroopers from the 1st squadron, transported by three SA-315B Lama and two SA-316B Alouette III helicopters, landed north of the village of Los Ramirez, 3km from the peak of El Roblar. They encountered little resistance and easily captured the summit. They then advanced on San José Guayabal where they were finally evacuated by truck. On the morning of 6 January, the infantry units set off, supported by 105mm howitzers. They slowly climbed the slopes of the Cerro and the fighting boiled down to a few skirmishes with the guerrillas fleeing. At the end of the operation, the FAES claimed to have destroyed three guerrilla camps, ammunition depots and other installations. The rebels would also have lost about 30 fighters whilst the FAES only had four wounded.[59] Nevertheless, after two days, the FAES withdrew and the FMLN combatants returned to their camps.

In early 1981, fighting between FAES and FMLN forces was also the result of guerrilla actions. Previously, on 2 January, FARN units had entered the Barrio de San Antonio Abad, west of the capital, where they built barricades and blocked roads before withdrawing. In response, the security forces and a FAES infantry company carried out security operations in the sector which allowed them to discover weapons and equipment and also the location of the FARN camp on the slopes of the San Salvador volcano. On the 4 January, units of the GN, the 1st Infantry Brigade and the 2nd Parachute Squadron supported by two Lama helicopters, advanced towards the volcano. They fell on the camp, where there were 100 men protected by mines and trenches. After an hour of fighting, the soldiers seized the first trenches and approached the command post. The guerrillas then exploded their stock of ammunition, causing a large fire allowing the fighters to escape but killing 27 people including six women. Thus, on the eve of the January offensive, the guerrilla forces planned to attack San Salvador from the west, were beaten and unable to act.[60] On 8 and 9 January, military operations also affected the Usulutan, La Union, San Vicente and Sonsonate departments.[61]

In the months preceding the January 1981 offensive, civil war set in. In the cities, the FMLN carried out occupations of factories and strikes in order to lead the social turmoil towards an insurrectionary situation, whilst the guerrillas spread in the countryside. The FMLN increased attacks on isolated FAES posts, eliminated government collaborators and informants in the areas where it established itself and installed its military forces.

4

THE JANUARY 1981 OFFENSIVE[1]

The election of Reagan in November 1980 was decisive for the strategy adopted by the FMLN and approved by Cuba. The CG was convinced that the new president would do everything possible to prevent the seizure of power by the FMLN and, as stated by the guerrilla commander Fermán Cienfuegos, 'The situation in El Salvador will be red hot by the time Mr. Reagan arrives. I think Mr. Reagan will find an irreversible situation in El Salvador by the time he reaches the presidency'.[2] The JRG had to therefore, fall before Reagan took office at the end of January.

Long an opponent of the military regime, the leader of the PDC, José Napoleon Duarte, joined the JRG which he took over in October 1980. It was in this position that he had to face the first nationwide offensive launched by the FMLN. (Authors Collection)

The plan of the offensive was drawn up by the FMLN and approved in Havana by Cuban officials including Castro on 13 and 14 December 1980. It consisted of three different and complementary sections. The first was the military offensive of the guerrilla forces, launched simultaneously against all the main garrisons of the FAES. The second was the launching of a national strike whose aim was to paralyse the whole country and prevent the government from reacting. The third was the organisation of mutiny in the ranks of the FAES. Part of the defecting soldiers would side with the guerrillas with their men and their weapons, strengthening the latter and weakening the defence of the government.[3]

Despite the precautions taken, the FMLN plans fall into the hands of the FAES but its commanders believed that this was a simple disinformation operation, seriously underestimating its adversary. The government and the military could not but be surprised when, on the night of 10 January 1981, the cables of all the international agencies broadcasted simultaneously in San Salvador and Mexico the FMLN communiqué which read: 'Today, at 5:00 p.m. afternoon, the general offensive began. The enemy is lost; we surrounded him; mob justice has arrived'.[4]

San Salvador

In the metropolis of San Salvador, the FMLN plan envisaged exploiting the social turmoil by infiltrating the poor neighbourhoods surrounding the capital, rallying the local militias responsible for building barricades and reinforcing the guerrilla columns coming from the outside. All these forces together had to besiege and overwhelm the FAES and the security forces installations with the support of the insurgent population.

On 5 January, the FMLN commanders in the capital received confirmation from the CG that the offensive had to begin on 10 January at 5.00 p.m. They could count on about a thousand fighters equipped with small arms with ammunition for only 3 days of combat. The guerrillas hoped to compensate this weakness by seizing weapons from the FAES and those provided by mutinous soldiers.[5]

The capital and its region were defended by the thousand soldiers of the 1st Infantry Brigade who were stationed in the San Carlos barracks located in the town of Mejicanos, under the orders of Colonel Manuel Edmundo Palacios. When the guerrillas entered in the suburbs, they distributed weapons and ammunition to locals, hoping to incite a popular uprising, but the citizenry mostly refused to participate, and the poorer citizens barricaded themselves in their homes.[6]

On the afternoon of 10 January, the 1st Infantry Brigade barracks became the target of small arms fire, bombs and some mortar fire. Troops of the 1st Infantry Brigade on patrol supported by an M-114 tankette, advanced in the main street of Mejicanos where they encountered a barricade. Other clashes took place during the day in Mejicanos and the guerrillas managed to resist, immobilising the FAES units. When night came, each side reinforced its positions. On the morning of the 11th, the guerrillas, armed with RPG-2 rocket launchers, attacked the Mejicanos barracks, which resisted. Finally, attacked from three sides by the 1st Infantry Brigade, the FMLN fighters had to abandon their

The M-114 APCs used to defeat the FMLN in San Salvador during the January 1981 offensive were second or third-hand log-dragging vehicles which had been bought in Georgia, USA. These were effectively a completely stripped M-114 Armoured Personnel Carrier with no weapons or armour of any kind. They were armed and armoured by FAES technicians. This M-114 was armed with a single M3 .50 calibre heavy machine gun mounted centrally just behind the cab. (Albert Grandolini Collection)

The January 1981 offensive was a shock for the soldiers who found themselves besieged in their barracks and had to fight hard to push back the FMLN fighters. (Albert Grandolini Collection)

barricades whilst the FAES entered Mejicanos where they gradually regained control.

Apopa was of major strategic importance for the FMLN as it was the location of the road that connected San Salvador to the west of the country and from where reinforcements could arrive to support the FAES in the capital. On 10 January, 200 FAL, ERP, FAR-LP and FARN fighters attacked the GN garrison whilst members of the FAL called on the population to join the insurrection. Whilst the GN and Civil Defence volunteers resisted in Apopa, forces of the 1st Infantry Brigade, the Artillery Brigade and the GN began to confront those of the FMLN responsible for preventing the arrival of reinforcements. These guerrilla forces were few in number and poorly armed. In Quezaltepeque, the 40 FMLN fighters were attacked by the Artillery Brigade arriving from San Juan Opico. The barricades were easily destroyed and FAES units broke into Apopa, forcing the guerrillas to withdraw. On the Troncal del Norte road which went towards Chalatenango, the FAL burnt four or five buses to block the way, but these barricades did not resist the arrival of troops from the security corps supported by an M-114. After a brief fight, the guerrillas fall back.[7]

In Soyapango, a locality where the FMLN was well established,[8] the main action of the guerrillas was the attack against the FAS Air Base in Ilopango carried out by the ERP. At 6:00 a.m. on 11 January, two 60mm mortars began to open fire on the airbase whilst 57mm recoilless rifles fired on runway eight. Another small force fired against the main entrance to the base. The soldiers retaliated and a jeep armed with a machine gun, scared away the rebels who were trying to shear the fence near the western entrance to the base. The paratroopers sent patrols wherever the guerrillas were present, and thanks to their experience, they easily prevailed. In Colonia Santa Lucia, the rebels ambushed the 2nd Airborne Squadron and the latter only succeeded in winning thanks to the arrival of reinforcements. They deployed around the base and after sometimes heavy fighting, forced the guerrillas to withdraw towards San Jacinto and Tonacatepeque.[9]

On 11 January, the FAES High Command General Staff declared a 7:00 p.m. to 5:00 a.m. curfew to curb guerrilla activities. The Cavalry Regiment under Major Oscar Campos Anaya, was deployed from La Libertad to eastern San Salvador to defend the capital from a guerrilla assault.[10]

From the south of the metropolis, in San Marcos, the FAPL special forces, which numbered 15 to 20 men, had to reach Cerro San Jacinto and then advance towards the FAS air base to participate in its attack. The incompetence of the commander of these special forces prevented them from taking action on 10 January. The next day, with a new commander, they tried to reach San Marcos but the energetic reaction of the FAES destroyed this project.[11] Throughout the night of 11 January, the 1st Infantry Brigade continued efforts to expel the FMLN from northern and eastern San Salvador.

In Soyapango, where the ERP command post in the capital was located under the orders of Commander Alejandro Montenegro, the locality was occupied by ERP and FARN fighters. The guerrillas used RPG-2s to attack the GN garrison whilst about 80 GNs split into three groups that went in different directions and confronted the barricades. One of the groups progressed to Colonia Los Flores where it dislodged the guerrillas from their positions. Another clashed in fierce combat with PRTC forces using RPG-2s and grenade launchers. The GNs were also fighting 2 PRTC platoons armed with RPG-2s, M-79 grenade launchers and Soviet hand grenades at Cuidad Delgado. The guerrillas managed to stop their progress, forcing them to use their HK-21 machine guns and G-3 grenades. The rebels were then forced to withdraw after having suffered heavy losses. They returned to Cuidad Delgado on 13 January, reinforced by militiamen to ambush a security force AML-90 tankette but again, suffered heavy losses.

On 14 January, the central PH garrison sent a detachment to reinforce the government forces fighting in Soyapango. It managed to reach the town hall of the city where it was joined by another section of the PH and a UR-416 APC. It then advanced towards the command post of the ERP which was defended by a barricade. The guerrillas managed to immobilise the UR-46 with a shot from the M-79 grenade launcher but they had to eventually withdraw. In the rest of Soyapango, the guerrillas continued to face the FAES who had the advantage of advancing under the protection of armoured vehicles. Commander Montenegro decided to occupy Tonacatepeque where the forces of the ERP attacked the GN garrison which resisted. Eventually, the FMLN retreated north in hopes of reaching Cerro Guazapa but many fighters, dressed in civilian clothes, quietly returned to their homes in San Salvador. At noon on 15 January, military intelligence warned that the FMLN would attack San Salvador's power grid later that night but no such attack occurred.[12]

In less than 24 hours, the guerrilla attacks in San Marcos, Soyapango, Ilopango and against the FAS Air Base, were broken by the FAES who suffered only light losses. On the side of the FMLN, there would have been about 150 killed whilst until March, the organisation lost about 50 percent of its personnel in the capital – victims of the repression.[13]

Santa Ana

In 1981, the city of Santa Ana in western El Salvador, with 180,000 inhabitants, was the second largest city in the country and an important economic centre. It was also a communication node connected to the border with Guatemala, the western part of the Chalatenango department, that of Sonsonate to the south and that of Ahuachapan to the west. It also housed the 2nd Infantry Brigade

The intervention of the AML-90s of the Cavalry Regiment prevented the city of Santa Ana from falling into the hands of the FMLN fighters. (Albert Grandolini Collection)

which included about a thousand soldiers under the command of Colonel Servio Tulio Figueora.

The FMLN was already active in Santa Ana where it continued to harass the garrison to train its fighters. In addition to Santa Ana, it had to seize other cities in the region, those of Metapan, Ciudad Arce, Armenia and Chalchuapa, eliminate the 2nd Brigade and the DM-7, occupy the port of Acajutla, seize the four border crossing points with Guatemala and block the Pan-American and Litoral Highways.

Since May 1980, the ERP had been in contact with various officers of the 2nd Infantry Brigade, Captain Mena Sandoval, Colonel Adino Cruz and Captain Marcelo Cruz who led a small group of officers favourable to the revolutionaries. Mena Sandoval was therefore, responsible for taking control of the 2nd Infantry Brigade garrison and tipping the soldiers to the side of the FMLN.

On the morning of 10 January, a group of ERP militants entered the Santa Ana garrison disguised as construction workers, whilst a dozen others were already in the 1st Infantry Company where they had arrived as recruits. Whilst outside the garrison, the columns of the FMLN invested the city, Sandoval brought together these militants and with the soldiers of the company he commanded, they tried to take control of the garrison. The operation was a failure and Sandoval finally made the decision to leave the burning garrison with 90 soldiers.[14]

In Santa Ana, there were still many areas occupied by the guerrillas, especially around the 2nd Infantry Brigade garrison and those of the security forces. Patrols from the 3rd company, the one that defeated Sandoval, tried to regain control of the city, supported by a Lama helicopter which nevertheless had to land after being hit by five bullets. According to the newspaper *El Pais*, another helicopter was shot down on the Pan-American highway.[15]

Since the morning of the 11th, troops from DM-6, DM-7 and the Cavalry Regiment arrived as reinforcements in Santa Ana. The FPL forces which blocked the Pan-American Highway that came from San Salvador, could not resist in front of the 1st section of the Cavalry Regiment. This included two Panhard AML and two APC UR-416 and had reached the 2nd Brigade garrison where reinforcements from DM-7 had already arrived. They received the order to support the troops fighting in the Apanteos district to the north of the city. The armoured vehicles were first pushed back by heavy fire and were ordered to retreat south. However, the AMLs 90mm guns could fire on a FMLN column moving on the slopes of Cerro Tecana. The guerrillas began to withdraw whilst the infantry and armoured vehicles consolidated their position. At the end of the day on 12 January, around 85 percent of the city was recaptured by the FAES.

The FMLN situation in Santa Ana became difficult and the ERP forces decided to withdraw towards Peñas Blancas further north. The column that took the road was led by Commander Raul. It included soldiers from Sandoval, some of whom then deserted the ranks of the guerrillas. On 14 January, the column finally arrived at Valle Nuevo north of Cutumay Camones where there was an FPL camp.[16]

Finally, the FAES regained control of Santa Ana. They set up roadblocks and checkpoints around the city whilst patrols circulated in its streets. They also launched search operations in areas of the region suspected of harbouring the guerrillas. It was in these circumstances that on 16 January, the FAES learned of the presence of 500 guerrillas in Cutumay Camones, including Sandoval and the soldiers who followed him. On the morning of the 17th, the 2nd Brigade discovered the defences of the ERP camp and violent fighting began. The arrival of reinforcements allowed the military to take the advantage and the rebels preferred to withdraw to the east. They then fall into an ambush by the 3rd Infantry Company. Sandoval and his group managed to flee on the morning of the 18th.[17] The fighting at Cutumay Camones was a disaster for the FMLN, with 97 combatants killed and a large quantity of weapons and materials lost.[18]

Chalatenango

The city of Chalatenango was the main economic centre in the north of the country and a major communication node to the north and east but also to the border with Honduras. In the city was the small DM-1 garrison of about 350 soldiers, some units of which were absent from the city where only 165 soldiers remained to defend the garrison under the command of Lieutenant Colonel José Dionisio Hernandez Castro.

Since 1977, the guerrillas had been very active in the Chalatenango department, where the FPL dominated. By 1980, the latter controlled many municipalities and worked hard to expand

A Magirus-based Mazinger at the head of a column with an M-60 machine gun fitted over the cab. (Albert Grandolini Collection)

their influence, establishing camps all around Chalatenango from which they launched almost daily attacks on the town. They were also active in the rest of the department where they harassed the small FAES and security forces garrisons. Thus, on 18 June 1980 between San José La Flores and Guarjila, the FPL ambushed a convoy of three military trucks, killing four soldiers.

At the end of 1980, commanders Douglas Santamaria and Jesus Rojas, as well as Domingo Vargas, an ex-Argentine soldier, arrived in Chalatenango to prepare the troops for the January offensive. On 26 December, the FPL with 500 to 1,000 fighters, carried out attacks against eight towns throughout the Chalatenango department. The fighting was particularly violent in Dulce Nombre de Jesus. The FAES had to send reinforcements supported by planes and helicopters to repel the guerrillas. They also destroyed four camps and a fortified FPL command post. On the 28th and 29th, the guerrillas again attacked a few small localities, the objective of the FPL being to form a liberated territory in Chalatenango. For the January offensive, they mobilised 350 armed and 300 unarmed fighters under the orders of Nicolas Hernan Solorzano Sanchez with the objective of seizing Chalatenango.

The guerrillas entered the city at night and meeting no resistance, took position to attack the DM-1 garrison. The fighting was violent and the forward defence positions of the FAES were captured by the guerrillas. The garrison then found itself besieged. Without the support of heavy weapons, the FPLs could nevertheless, not penetrate the garrison, which resisted all night. In the morning, Lieutenant Colonel Dionisio launched an offensive action north of the barracks using a Mazinger, a civilian Magirus-Deutz-Jupiter truck reinforced with armour. His appearance surprised the guerrillas and the FAES regained the initiative. Due to its numerical superiority, the firepower of the military forced the FPL to retreat. Commander Santamaria ordered a retreat towards El Jicaro and on the morning of the 12th, the guerrillas had completely evacuated Chalatenango.[19]

At the announcement of the attack against the DM-1 garrison, the forces of the 4th Infantry Brigade set out from the base of El Paraiso to come to its aid. The vanguards met the forces of the FPL installed on the road to prevent the arrival of reinforcements. After a first fight, the soldiers were pushed back and a Mazinger was immobilised by the explosion of a mine. The soldiers received support from an Alouette III helicopter which machine-gunned the insurgents. New reinforcements from the 4th Brigade arrived and fired heavily on the FPL positions. At 10:00 a.m. an airborne force landed and with the units already present, began to surround the rebels who managed to escape towards Upatoro.

The FPL lost about 45 fighters in Chalatenango including Roberto Lira Morel, a member of the Chilean CP whilst 300 deserted who, for the most part, took refuge in Mesa Grande in Honduras. The DM-1 counted six soldiers killed and 10 injured.[20] The FMLN also attempted to capture the Cerron Grande Hydroelectric Dam in Chalatenango and Cabañas Departments which generated power, but the operation failed.[21]

Zacatecoluca and San Vicente

The La Paz, San Vicente and La Cabaña departments depended on the Paracentral Front. In these regions dominated by coffee growing, guerrilla forces recruited easily. The FPL were the most powerful organisation and since 1979 there had been almost daily clashes against the DM-5 forces based in San Vicente and those of the *Centro de Instruccion de Ingenieros de la Fuerza Armada* (Armed Force Engineers Training Centre or CIIFA) in Zacatecoluca which were numerically low.

For the January offensive, the Paracentral Front aimed to take control of the entire San Vicente department and part of La Paz as well as the Pan-American and Litoral Highways and two bridges over the Lempa River to prevent the arrival of reinforcements from and towards San Salvador. The FPL had many camps in the region and its command led by Juan Méndez, settled in Paz Opico. In the Cerros de San Pedro, north of San Vicente, there were PRTC camps which had about 100 fighters armed with Galil rifles and Lewis machine guns and also the ERP forces. The Paracentral Front was the only one to have a joint operations directorate for all the member organisations of the FMLN. The troops were well armed since they had benefited greatly from arms shipments from Cuba and Nicaragua, including M-70 grenade launchers and RPG-2 rocket launchers. Their first objective was Zacatacoluca.

Zacatecoluca, capital of the La Paz department, was located between the Pan-American and Litoral Highways which crossed the whole country. This situation gave it an important strategic role for both the FMLN and the FAES. On the military level, the city had been home to the CIIFA since 1964, commanded by Colonel Marco Aurelio Gonzales and had 191 soldiers and 14 officers, as well as three armoured vehicles, an M-114, a Mazinger and a Magirus-Deutz-Jupiter truck reinforced with armour.[22]

The FMLN forces set off on the evening of 10 January. At the entrance to Zacatecoluca, a guerrilla truck came across a PN checkpoint. A firefight ensued, which put the garrison on alert. The element of surprise was lost and the guerrillas quickly found themselves in difficulty. The fight also began around the CIIFA garrison where the guerrillas installed *rampas*, 'artillery without cannon', home-made and capable of launching a medium-sized explosive charge at 25 to 30 metres. However, the shots from the *rampas* were imprecise and those which touched the goal failed to destroy the iron gates of the barracks. Nevertheless, the firefight did not weaken and the guerrilla groups tried to destroy the trenches which defended the garrison. Later, the CIIFA soldiers came out with two tankettes. An M-114 was hit by a rocket.[23]

The FPL unit, which was to attack the barracks from the east, fell halfway on a FAES patrol which had established a barrage on a bridge. It tried to cross it but it was stopped by an HK-21 machine

The FAS used Fouga Magister since 1970. They were used for purely military ends and thus, were armed with machine guns. They were useful for the counter-insurgency fight until 1983, the date of their withdrawal. (Albert Grandolini Collection)

gun which caused a dozen deaths. The group arriving from the west also failed to reach the garrison to support the attack, whilst the two platoons responsible for neutralising the municipal police, were immobilised by fighting without having reached their objective. At dusk, CIIFA forces supported by two tankettes, broke the lines of the guerrillas, which nevertheless managed to withdraw towards Palo Grande to the north of the city. The various FMLN attacks on Zacatecoluca therefore, ended in failure. It lost 60 killed and 30 wounded whilst the FAES and the security forces had 12 soldiers, and one GN killed and 18 soldiers wounded.

The FPL command decided to launch a new attack on Zacatecoluca from Palo Grande to the north of the city. On the morning of the 13 January, three sections of 45 fighters each launched the assault but were stopped by the FAES. The guerrillas could no longer advance and retreated towards the volcano of San Vicente.[24]

In the rest of the department, the guerrillas attacked the GN garrison at San Nicolas Lempa using RPG-2s. The GNs resisted for two hours until reinforcements arrived. At Tecoluca, on the Litoral Highway, two FPL platoons ambushed a joint GN and DM-5 patrol. In the afternoon, new reinforcements from the DM-5 failed to cross the roadblock that the guerrillas had set up on the road. On the 11th, the latter seized the town hall of Tecoluca then attacked the GN garrison but without success. Two Alouette III helicopters even managed to land to evacuate wounded GNs whilst an Ouragan fighter-bomber and Fouga Magister fighters came to support the besieged garrison. It was finally a caterpillar tankette which managed to cross the roadblocks, accompanied by reinforcements from the DM-5. After two hours of fighting, the guerrillas were defeated but managed to leave Tecoluca.

The GN post was attacked in San Esteban Catarina by 40 to 60 FAL and PRTC fighters who, on the morning of the 12th, controlled the small town. Nevertheless, in the afternoon, reinforcements from the DM-5, with the support of mortars and machine guns, recaptured it. In San Sebastian, two FAL platoons entered the town to attack the GN post. The fighting lasted all day on the 11th without the post falling and the guerrillas finally withdrew. The GN post of San Lorenzo, north-east of San Vicente, was attacked by PRTC forces. At dusk, the defenders managed to withdraw and the guerrillas remained in the locality until 13 January. In Apastepeque, the fighting was extremely violent and five members of the Territorial Service and a GN agent were killed whilst 45 members of the Territorial Service were missing. Nevertheless, the guerrillas did not manage to impose themselves there either. In Santa Clara, the GN post was besieged all day but the guerrillas lacked ammunition whilst the besieged were supplied by a Lama helicopter. The next day, the GNs were forced to retreat.

In San Vicente, two FAL platoons descended from the San Vicente volcano to reach the station to the east of the city and then advanced on the DM-5 garrison. They were stopped by a military patrol, and after a skirmish, they withdrew. FPL forces meanwhile approached from the south but quickly withdrew.

At the announcement of the FMLN offensive and after having averted all danger in San Vicente, the DM-5, commanded by Colonel Napoleon Alvarado, sent the 2nd Company to rescue Zacatecoluca. It felt into an ambush south-west of San Vicente, but this action could only delay the soldiers, not prevent them from reaching Zacatecoluca on 11 January where the fighting had already stopped. The 2nd section of the armoured squadron with two AMLs and two UR-416s was sent to reinforce the units controlling the Quebrada Seca bridge and that of Cuscatlan on the Lempa River. Along the way, it was ambushed. It remained under guerrilla fire for three hours before reaching the Quebrada Seca bridge. For the next 22 days, it conducted a mobile surveillance of the bridges whilst the PRTC forces in the Cerros de San Pedra were unable to take any action.[25]

Morazan Department

The FMLN was particularly well established in the north of the Morazan department where there were many ERP camps which were used to provide military and political training but also as a support and supply structure. There was also a small zone dominated by the FARN which had four platoons. This FMLN implantation, led

The Morazan department was an ERP stronghold which controlled several sectors well before the January 1981 offensive. On the banner is written: 'Morazan: land liberated. Defend our land!' (Albert Grandolini Collection)

Although the guerrillas had quality armament as shown by these fighters, some of whom were armed with an M-16 rifle, the lack of coordination and communication between its units led to the failure of the January offensive. (Albert Grandolini Collection)

since November 1980 by Jorge Antonio Meléndez Lopez, allowed it to form platoons comprising approximately 25 men each who benefited from arms shipments arrived by sea but also by road from the Colomoncagua camp in Honduras. Despite the blows suffered in October 1980 during Operation Rayovac, they multiplied ambushes, especially on the road linking Gotera to Perquin. With a thousand fighters at the beginning of 1981, the objective was to seize San Francisco Gotera, the capital of the department, a mission entrusted to William Pascasio.[26]

Whilst San Francisco Gotera was a modest city of only 10,000 inhabitants, it was also the main economic centre of the Morazan department and the presence of a small airstrip at Chilanga 3km to the north gave it a certain strategic importance. On the military level, the city had been home since 1975 to the Commando company of the FAES and the CICFA commanded by Lieutenant Colonel José Alejandro Cisneros, whose recruits were all volunteers and had already completed their military service.[27] However, this unit only had 180 soldiers who also had the obligation to hold defensive positions in Perquin and in Cerro Cacahuatique. The low numbers and their dispersal made the city particularly vulnerable in the face of a large scale action, especially since the soldiers would not be able to receive reinforcements before 48 hours and they had to retain control of the airstrip and the CA-7 road.[28]

On the morning of 12 January, a section of the ERP commanded by Julio Guevara, launched a frontal attack against the Chilanga airstrip while two other sections attacked from the north and the south. The airstrip was badly defended by too weak manpower. It was quickly captured by the guerrillas with the exception of the control tower. The FAS sent an Arava equipped with three 12.7mm machine guns and 14 rockets to support the commandos defending it. Arriving above Chilanga, the Aravas was hit by bullets but managed to fire its rockets before returning to Ilopango. The FAS then decided to send two Alouette helicopters to the 3rd Infantry Brigade in San Miguel to support the reinforcements intended for San Francisco Gotera.[29]

The sound of fighting around the airstrip was heard by the San Francisco Gotera garrison, which went on alert as the ERP forces entered the city and advanced in its direction. On the morning of the 12th, after some machine guns and a rocket launcher fired against the barracks, Pascasio's forces launched an assault. It came up against heavy fire from the defenders. Other attempts were also unsuccessful. The resistance of the Commandos seemed to waver when a small group of guerrillas managed to approach 10 metres from the enclosure. The Commandos then received support from Lama and Alouette helicopters which machine-gunned the guerrillas and took advantage of this to launch counterattacks. One of these attacks made it possible to recapture the lost defensive positions and the Commandos continued to advance. The guerrillas, disconcerted, broke up and Pascasio's forces lost their coherence. On the airstrip, the guerrillas seized the last entrenchment of the military – the control tower.[30]

The Commandos had managed to loosen the grip of the guerrillas and they returned to their defensive positions when night fall and awaited a new assault at dawn. On the morning of 13 January, Pascasio launched a new attack against the PN positions. The police were well entrenched and received the help of two Fougas which dropped four bombs. meanwhile, at the announcement of the attack on San Francisco Gotera, the 3rd Infantry Brigade sent one of its sections, reinforced by troops from the DM-3, the PN, an M-114 tankette and a Mazinger.

On the morning of 13 January, these reinforcements surprised the troops of Javier Negro charged with preventing their arrival. The latter opened fire against the soldiers who were supported by two Alouette helicopters. When ammunition ran out, the guerrillas fled in disorder. If the DM-3 troops returned to their barracks, the others continued their march on San Francisco Gotera. They resumed the airstrip with the help of the Alouettes whilst the fighting continued in the city. The M-114 and the Mazinger routed the forces led by Heleno Castro as Lama helicopters and Rallye planes flew over the town to indicate to ground troops the direction of the guerrilla retreat. Afraid of being surrounded, Pascasio ordered the evacuation of all rebel forces. A section of paratroopers supported by two Alouettes, launched a pursuit against the guerrillas and the fighting continued for a few more days further north in the Morazan department. Finally, the fighting for San Francisco Gotera caused the death of 30 rebels with 50 wounded whilst the FAES counted nine dead and 18 wounded.[31]

Usulutan

In the Usulatan department, one of the richest in the country thanks to the cultivation of coffee, the south-eastern front had the mission of taking control of the southern zone of the San Miguel, Usulatan and La Union departments, in effect the coastal area between Jiquilisco and the Gulf of Fonseca, taking advantage of the immobilisation of FAES forces caused by the attacks on the towns of San Miguel, Usulutan and La Union. The ERP, led politically by Claudio Rabindranath Armijo Serrano and militarily by Commander Francisco Gonzalo Martinez, was the dominant force. In addition to the ERP, the Front included FAR-LP forces under the orders of Oscar Alberto Miranda Flamenco, the FARN commanded by Ramon Medico and the FAPL installed in the region of Lempa and La Montañita.

The FAES took the FMLN by surprise by acting on 8 January 1981 with an offensive in the areas of Jiquilisco, San Marcos Lempa and the canton of La Mora. These regions were bombarded by 81mm mortars, forcing the FAR-LP to move north where the military organised an ambush. The guerrillas lost 13 men but managed to withdraw. FMLN forces in San Marcos de Lempa and La Mora canton fled north or south, pursued by fire from a FAS Arava. They would not be able to participate in the 10 January operation.

On the morning of 11 January, the guerrillas advanced on the DM-4 garrison from the south and west of Usulutan. To come to their aid, the FAES decided to organise an airborne operation by disembarking from a C-47, the 35 soldiers of the reinforced section of the 2nd Airborne Squadron on an airstrip 2km west of Usulutan.

Guerrilla fighters in 1981. (Albert Grandolini Collection)

The operation went smoothly and the paratroopers advanced on the town without difficulty. They fell on the rear of the FARN who resisted, house after house. The ERP forces, coming from the west and reaching the centre of Usulutan where they attacked the PN barracks, heard fighting between the FARN and the paratroopers. They decided to fall back whilst the paratroopers continued to advance, now supported by a Mazinger equipped with three 20mm cannons. Eventually, the FMLN retreated east to Jucuaran. Paratroopers stayed in the town for five days after three were killed and 12 injured.

Further east, La Union was home to the National Navy base and was therefore an important but perilous target with its 150 soldiers and seven patrol boats. The city was also the headquarters of the DM-3, under the command of Lieutenant Colonel Ramon Antonio Morales Ruiz, which only had an infantry company and a support company equipped with Browning machine guns and 81mm ECIA mortars.

ERP forces, led by Claudio Armijo in the Jucuaran sector, were to attack La Union from the west and southwest using the Litoral Highway, whilst from El Carmen, another force led by Circunsion Claros joined by a platoon of the FAL, also had to attack La Union. The 300 fighters of Armijo set out on the morning of 11 January but they get lost on the way and found themselves, on the morning of the 13th, in the Gualoso sector. At this time, two patrols of the DM-3 discovered them by chance. The first FAES patrol was annihilated whilst the second retreated. Reinforcements from the DM-3 nevertheless arrived in the area and the fighting resumed. Eventually, Armijo decided to retreat to Jucuaran. The troop led by Claros set

The security forces were particularly targeted by the actions of the FMLN during the January 1981 offensive and had to fight hard to avoid defeat. (Albert Grandolini Collection)

out from El Carmen and a day late, began the encirclement of the naval base. It quickly confronted FAES patrols before withdrawing.

On Villalobos' orders, Armijo tried to attack La Union again. He took a new route to approach the town but the guerrillas were discovered by the soldiers and had to flee again. Another small ERP group was discovered at Cerro El Jiote by DM-3 forces. With the help of the FAS which bombarded the place, the guerrillas were driven out after having lost 25 fighters. ERP forces took refuge on the slopes of the Conchagua volcano with the mission of maintaining pressure on La Union and opening a route to receive the supplies sent from Nicaragua.[32]

In the Rest of El Salvador

On 10 January, the FMLN launched smaller actions in the rest of El Salvador with the aim of immobilising as many government forces as possible. This was the case of those carried out by the Central Zone of the FPL whose command was installed in the Cerro de Guazapa. The FPL attacked Aguilares, Ingenio La Cabaña, Guazapa, in the north of San Salvador department, Ilobasco, Valle Victoria and Jutiapa in that of La Cabaña, Tenancingo in that of Cuscatlan but each time they were repelled. They also sought to seize Cinquera, a small town in the La Cabaña department. They then came up against the resistance of the local GN which gradually received reinforcements from the surrounding towns with the support of a Lama helicopter and then an Arava equipped with rockets. The guerrillas were driven out of their positions.

From Cerro de Guazapa, forces of the RN, FPL, PCS and PRTC also aimed to seize Suchitoto and other secondary objectives. Among the latter, the guerrillas seized Oratorio de Concepcion on the 10th but failed on the 11th to capture Tonacatepeque. At Suchitoto, the FAPL encountered resistance from the small PN and GN garrisons and had to withdraw.

In Chalchuapa, on the border with Guatemala, on the morning of 10 January, three platoons of FPL, ERP and FAL, in effect 60 to 75 combatants, attacked the PN garrison. The fights lasted all day. The next day reinforcements from Sonsonate's DM-6 began to reach the area around Chalchuapa. On the 12th, an armoured unit arrived which included an AML forcing the FMLN to withdraw after having lost 22 combatants whilst four policemen were killed.[33]

North of Santa Ana, near the border with Guatemala, Metapan was a communication node defended by a weak garrison of less than 20 PN and GN agents. The town was attacked on the morning of the 11th by the FPL and the FAL. At the beginning of the afternoon, a GN patrol coming from Santa Ana to rescue its defenders, was ambushed. The FAS then sent a Lama helicopter to supply the defenders who lacked ammunition. When it tried to land, it was caught under guerrilla fire and had to land urgently near Santa Rosa in Guatemala. On the morning of the 12th, the guerrillas finally abandoned Metapan. The operation claimed the lives of 12 rebels whilst five PN members died and two were injured. The next days, the 2nd Infantry Brigade also secured Metapan with the support of the Recruit Instruction Centre and the Artillery Brigade.[34]

Santa Rosa de Lima, a communication node that connected San Francisco Gotera to the north-west, the port of La Union to the south-east and the Honduran border to the north-east, was attacked by two FARN platoons whilst a third blocked the road that led to Agua Caliente. The city was only defended by two posts of the GN and the PN which brought together only 20 to 25 agents. The security forces refused to surrender and the fighting continued until the morning of the 12th when reinforcements from San Miguel arrived, supported by a helicopter and two FAS combat planes. At the end of the day, the guerrillas left the city.[35]

The Results of the January 1981 Offensive

The January offensive marked a turning point in the Salvadoran crisis. The FMLN attacked 43 different locations succeeding in temporarily occupying four capitals of departments, about 20 towns and villages and besieging the FAES and the GN garrisons in many places. It even attacked the FAS base in Ilopango. These actions which affected the whole country, obliged the FAES to take the first place in the fight against the FMLN, a task which until then, was essentially devolved to the security forces.[36] The Salvadoran conflict shifted definitively from the realm of public order to that of military conflict.

Despite the scale of the offensive it led, the FMLN suffered a setback with multiple causes. The surprise effect was zero, the FMLN had never hidden its intention to launch a major operation since December 1980 – of which the intelligence services were informed. Only the national scale of the January offensive surprised the authorities. The main military weakness of the FMLN was nevertheless, the lack of coordination, both at the local level where the troops were not used in a coherent manner and at the national level, where it did not succeed in launching simultaneous attacks. It lacked a unified command and common tactical objectives,

Arava IAI 201 transporters were widely used to carried reinforcements but these aircraft were vulnerable to guerrilla fire. (Albert Grandolini Collection)

each guerrilla organisation directing only its own forces with no cooperation between them.

The FMLN also lacked heavy armament. In the attack on the FAES barracks, it could only conduct sieges, without ever succeeding in destroying the walls or neutralising the defences. Finally, the fighters only had the experience of urban guerrilla warfare carried out during the 1970s, which was not sufficient to confront a regular army in the open. Despite the training of FMLN cadres in Cuba, Nicaragua or Lebanon and the receipt of modern weapons, the need to act before Reagan could come to the aid of the JRG did not leave the guerrillas sufficient time to prepare. Commanders were inexperienced in the tactical conduct of war operations, whilst combatants lacked knowledge in the use of modern weapons such as grenade launchers, RPG-2s, machine guns and mortars.[37]

Above all, the initial plan of the FMLN was based on the idea that an insurrection was the way to overcome the inferiority, both numerical and qualitative, of the guerrillas. On 13 January, the FDR called for Salvadorans to go on a general strike to support the FMLN's offensive. Duarte called on Salvadorans to ignore the FMLN and continue to work, promising that the FAES would protect them. Only 20,000 Salvadorans from 26 factories went on strike, most of them in isolated areas in or near major cities.[38] This national strike, intended to paralyse the country, was a failure. Convinced that the population supported it massively, the FMLN badly organised the insurrection, leaving its preparation to mass organisations which were stripped of their main leaders who left to join the guerrillas. Nevertheless, the main reason for this absence of uprising was the refusal of the population for the military solution to the crisis of the country proposed by the FMLN.[39]

Another major component of the FMLN plan yielded even more disastrous results. The FAES remained loyal to the government and the ambition of the revolutionaries to provoke mutinies failed, despite the efforts of the ERP which, since 1977, had formed a team responsible for infiltrating the garrisons of the capital and contacting soldiers, which the RN also did.[40] The only success in January 1981 occurred at the 2nd Brigade garrison in Santa Ana where Captains Francisco Mena Sandoval and Marcelo Cruz defected to lead their company.

The cohesion of the FAES did not break, the soldiers reacting quickly to repel the guerrillas in a few hours, taking advantage of the experience they possessed. Nevertheless, the January offensive showed some FAES weaknesses. The only strategic reserves they had were the Cavalry Regiment and the Airborne units sent to save the 2nd Infantry Brigade and the CIIFA. If desperate situations had arisen elsewhere, the FAES would not have been able to regain the initiative. On the equipment level, the use of RPG-2 by the FMLN posed a risk for the armoured vehicles and only the incompetence of the rebels in their use, made it possible to avoid a disaster. The FAS also played a role in supporting ground units, but in January 1981, six helicopters were temporarily out of service, in effect 60 percent of FAS personnel, while two Arava IAI 201 transporters were hit by bullets during combat. Fighter planes played a minimal role except for the armed Fouga. In the end, the action of the FAS was not decisive, a lot of bombardment did not reach the goal and the land-air coordination was poor. Only the use of helicopters was effective, but their prolonged intervention ran the risk of being hit by guerrilla fire.[41]

The failure of the offensive was a trauma for the FMLN. If it publicly announced that this setback was above all, tactical rather than strategic and was explained in particular by the lack of training and experience of the guerrilla forces, the crisis was much deeper. The RN decided to suspend its military actions whilst the ERP planned to withdraw its troops to Nicaragua. The FPL and the PCS thought for their part, that the guerrillas had to abandon the countryside, demobilise and return to the cities until the situation was more favourable.[42] On 26 January, the leaders of the FMLN conceded that the offensive had not sparked the national uprising for which they had hoped. They had believed that their actions against the government would spark a 'full-scale popular revolution' and that several garrisons would mutiny, as had happened in Nicaragua two years earlier.[43] The FMLN thus recognised that it did not have the military capacity to seize power, nor the sufficient force to trigger a popular insurrection. In a private interview, a senior FMLN commander even noted that 'if the enemy had been well prepared, effective and coordinated, we would have been annihilated'.[44]

According to different estimates, in January 1981, around 12,000 members of the FAES and law enforcement forces clashed with around 3,700 guerrillas and 5,000 FMLN militiamen. The fighting, from 10 to 19 January, would cost the lives of 980 rebels and 142 soldiers, the most important losses taking place in Santa Ana and San Fernando Gotera. The regions around these cities as well as those of Zacatecoluca and Chalatenango were the most affected by the fighting, causing the departure to Honduras of about 5,000 civilians.[45]

5
THE RESISTANCE OF THE FMLN, 10 JANUARY 1981 TO MID-1982

If the General Offensive of January 1981 did not allow the FMLN to obtain the military rout of the government, the FAES did not obtain any strategic victories either. The war was long-lasting and faced with this situation, the FMLN gradually adopted the strategy of a protracted people's war which it called 'resist, grow and advance'. It was based on the constitution of a liberated territory in the northern and north-eastern regions of the country near the Honduran border whilst the military controlled the cities and the west of El Salvador. This partition of the country was conducive to the development of a war of movements whilst the new Reagan administration decided to support the FAES in their fight against the FMLN.

Reagan and Military Support in El Salvador

Just before leaving office on 14 January, President Carter resumed sending military aid to the JRG and authorised aid of US$5 million including the supply of rifles, ammunition, grenade launchers, uniforms, jeeps, trucks, light artillery and six UH-1H helicopters which were delivered on 16 January.[1]

US Ambassador Deane R Hinton arrived in El Salvador after Ronald Reagan's election. He was responsible for implementing the policy of the new administration in this country. (Albert Grandolini Collection)

On 20 January 1981, Ronald Reagan was sworn in as President of the United States. For his administration, the US faced a grave threat to their national security in Central America. Reagan told Congress on 27 April 1983:

> Nearness on the map does not even begin to tell the strategic importance of Central America, bordering as it does on the Caribbean – our lifeline to the outside world. 2/3 of all our foreign trade and petroleum pass through the Panama Canal and the Caribbean. In a European crisis, at least 1/2 of our supplies for NATO would go through these areas at sea.[2]

He believed that Carter let communism spread in the region without doing anything and that the Sandinista victory in Nicaragua could cause a domino effect of which El Salvador was the first victim, a prospect considered unacceptable. This ideological vision of the Salvadoran conflict would determine all the policy of the new administration although it denied its local roots. It marked a major turning point as noted in his memoirs, Duarte wrote:

> US pressure and aid, on a scale we had never imagined, began pouring into El Salvador a month after Reagan's inauguration. When Secretary of State Alexander Haig decided to draw his line against international communism through El Salvador, our problems suddenly became the world's problem. The long and bloody struggle between the Salvadoran Right, Leftist guerrillas and Christian Democrats became a metaphor for the East-West struggle.[3]

A first option for the Reagan administration would be to send troops to El Salvador, but Congress, the Pentagon and above all most Americans, were reluctant to face this solution which might recall the Vietnamese trauma. The second, more modest, consisted in the implementation of a counter-insurgency strategy also called Low Intensity Conflict, suggesting an implication below the threshold of a conventional armed conflict. It was this last option that was chosen and filtered down to Washington by sending small groups of special forces to train the FAES and providing economic and military aid. In February 1981, the Reagan administration provided emergency military aid of US$25 million to El Salvador and the dispatch of new military advisors, without the approval of Congress. In March, it authorised the CIA to carry out covert operations in Nicaragua with the aim of putting an end to the supply of arms to the Salvadoran guerrillas.[4]

The US counter-insurgency strategy rested on several pillars, political, economic and military. Economic and political reforms appeared essential to redress the situation of the country in order to eliminate the imbalances that fuelled discontent and conversely, demonstrated the credibility of the government. One of the most important moments of this strategy had to be the holding of the Constituent Assembly elections in 1982.

On a military level, the Americans were concentrating on the modernisation and professionalisation of the FAES. For Washington, this aspect was essential since it had to allow it

President Reagan's determination to prevent the victory of the FMLN in El Salvador transformed a conflict with local roots into a battlefield of the Cold War. (Albert Grandolini Collection)

Following the war with Honduras in 1969, El Salvador was placed under a strict arms embargo by the USA and experienced significant problems with the acquisition of heavy arms. A few UMB-59 mortars, a few M55 anti-aircraft guns calibre 20mm, and a few artillery pieces were acquired from Yugoslavia. However, the bulk of armour consisted of a handful of obsolete M3A1 Stuart light tanks, most of which were non-operational, and about 20 Rayos: improvised armoured trucks based on the M35 REO chassis. It was only in preparations for the Miss Universe contest that 10 unarmed AR-416 armoured personnel carriers on UNIMOG chassis, were acquired from West Germany. All were originally painted in dark green and although wearing the insignia of the Guardia Nacional, served with the sole Cavalry Regiment of the Army. (Artwork by David Bocquelet)

As soon as the insurgency of the FMLN erupted, tankers of the Cavalry Regiment took care to camouflage their AR-416s with splotches of sand and light green colour, as illustrated here. Moreover, several were re-armed with Browning M3 machine guns calibre 7.62mm. When President Carter reinforced the arms embargo upon El Salvador, Salvadorians purchased 27 tracked Woodmaster log haulers from the USA and under the direction of Captain Oswaldo Marenco, converted them into armoured vehicles patterned after German AR-416s. By 1980, a similar modification was applied in form of the Mazzinger-Z armoured commercial trucks, the design of which proved less successful. (Artwork by David Bocquelet)

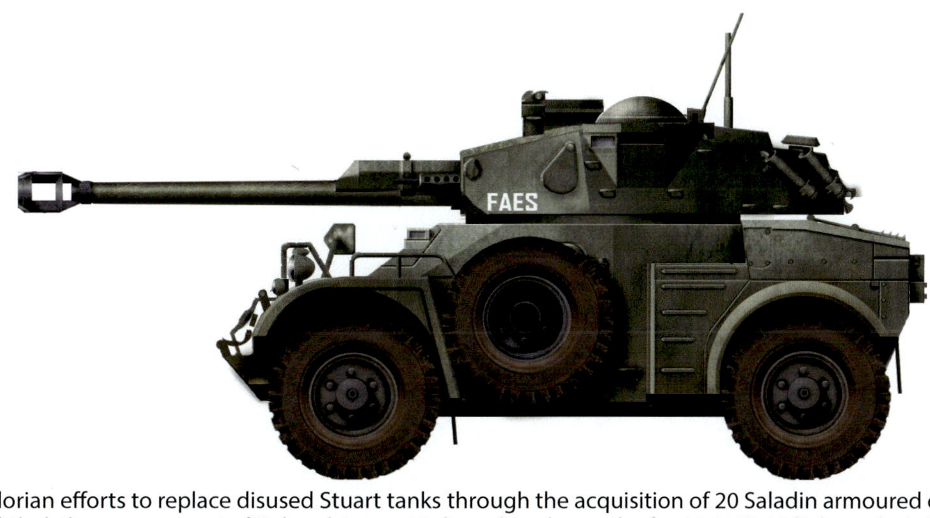

Once Salvadorian efforts to replace disused Stuart tanks through the acquisition of 20 Saladin armoured cars from Great Britain had failed, the government of Colonel Arturo Molina placed an order for 12 AMX-13 light tanks in France, in 1975. Although the money was, reportedly, transferred to Paris, not one was delivered – meaning it was either stolen without any acquisition or the tanks were diverted and sold off to somebody else. Instead, El Salvador eventually acquired 12 Panhard AML-90 armoured cars, equipped with the D921 F1 gun calibre 90mm. (Artwork by David Bocquelet)

Like AR.416s, AML-90s – the heaviest-armed combat vehicles of the sole Cavalry Regiment of the Salvadorian Army as of 1979 – were originally painted in dark green overall. By the end of the year, most had received similar camouflage pattern in two shades of light green. The terrain of El Salvador proved anything else than ideal for armoured vehicle, the FAES AML-90s saw lots of action, and were subsequently reinforced by 10 AML-60s and 10 Panhard M3 VTT armoured personnel carriers. (Artwork by David Bocquelet

As the civil disorder grew in the late 1970s and the widespread use of nail traps and small IEDs quickly crippled many wheeled vehicles of the FAES, unable to acquire tracked armoured vehicles from abroad, the Army acquired 27 log-dragging vehicles based on the stripped-down chassis of M114 APCs acquired from Georgia, USA. Four were in such a poor condition that they could be used as sources of spares only; a team led by Captain Oswaldo Marenco converted the other 23 into armoured personnel carriers through adding a large, rectangular box body, very similar to the original M114 design. (Artwork by David Bocquelet)

During the work on 23 of his APCs, Marenco refined his design: as well as providing the driver with a pair of thick, square, bullet-proof glass windscreens at the front (protected by a large rectangular flap that could be folded over these), he added three rectangular vision blocks down the side of the superstructure. Access to the vehicle was by the means of a large rectangular door at the back and four hatches on the top. By early 1980, armament was added. FAES 10001 received a single HK.21 machine gun over the rear right side of the vehicle; FAES 10002 had two mounting points for HK.21 light machine guns, while most of subsequent examples received a pintle-mounted M3 machine gun. (Artwork by David Bocquelet)

Established back in 1917 with some help from Mexico, the Fuerza Aeerea Savladorena is one of oldest air forces in Latin America. During the 1970s, it experienced similar embargo related problems with acquisition of new equipment similar to the FAES but managed to acquire a small number (up to five) of Aerospatiale SA.315B Lama light helicopters from French sources. This example, construction number 2455, was operated by the Ilopango-based Escuadrón de Helicópteros in white and dark-green livery, serial 13 and the nickname 'Tazumal'. It was written off on 4 April 1980, when the pilot landed it at El Amatal beach and forgot about the high tide, as a consequence of which it was swept away by the sea, causing irreparable damage. (Artwork by Luca Canossa)

In late 1981 or early 1982, surviving Lamas – meanwhile operated by the Ilopango-based Grupo de Combate – received a camouflage pattern in dark sand and dark olive green. The helicopter with construction number 2442, nicknamed 'Atonal', thus lost its nickname and looked like this, wearing only the FAS serial 12. Lamas were highly appreciated for their 'hot and high' performance, and saw intensive deployment for casualty evacuation, communication, reconnaissance and utility purposes. (Artwork by Luca Canossa)

This Aerospatiale SE.316B Alouette III of the FAS had the construction number 5393. It was painted in olive green overall and wore only the serial 24: this artwork shows it around 1980, by when it was operated by the Grupo de Combate, from Ilopango. As far as is known, it was never armed. (Artwork by Luca Canossa)

As of 1982, this Hughes/McDonnell MD.500D helicopters of the FAS was still wearing a 'rather civilian' livery in white and bright red. Having a construction number 600746D, it was nicknamed the 'Guardiancillo', and wore a large black FAS serial 32, while operated by the Escuadrón de Helicópteros from Ilopango AB. It is shown with the left cockpit door in open position. (Artwork by Luca Canossa)

Another of FAS Hughes/McDonnell MD.500s in around 1982 was this example: the construction number 410928D, FAS serial 34, painted in white and dark blue. By this point in time, none of the MD.500s were armed: instead, the Escuadrón de Helicópteors flew them from Ilopango AB for visual reconnaissance or for casualty evacuation and utility purposes. (Artwork by Luca Canossa)

This formerly Israeli Fouga CM.170 Magister (powered by Marbore II engines) had the construction number D27 and was delivered to El Salvador on 15 June 1975. It received the serial 507 and a camouflage pattern in tan and two shades of green on top surfaces, while undersurfaces were painted in light grey and it was assigned to the Escuadrón de Caza y Bombardeo. It is shown as of 1980, armed with two 70kg bombs of Israeli origin and two nose-mounted 7.62mm machine guns. (Artwork by Luca Canossa)

Another notable CM.170 Magister of the FAS from the early times of the war in El Salvador was this example: construction number 43, formerly serving with the French Air Force, before receiving the serial 510 in Salvadorian service. It was powered by Marbore VI engines and delivered to the FAS on 26 April 1979. Originally not armed, it received two 7.62mm machine guns in the nose and is shown armed with four Matra F2 pods for unguided rockets calibre 68mm installed (two under each wing). Notably, instead of a roundel, it received a 'fin flash' on the rear of engine nacelles. (Artwork by Luca Canossa)

MD.450 Ouragans of the FAS were already flown intensively before the war. This example, serial 705, was operated by the Escuadrón de Caza y Bombardeo from Ilopango AB, and is shown as of 1979, with its camouflage pattern in tan and two shades of green already in worn out condition. Usually flown by Colonel Oscar N. Bolanos, FAS 705 was maintained by the crew led by Dolores R. Castro, which applied a big shark mouth insignia on its nose and is shown with its drop tanks removed from wing-tips. (Artwork by Luca Canossa)

Another notable Ouragan of the Escuadrón de Caza y Bombardeo, FAS from the 1970s was this example: serial 715, on which the ground crew, led by Cabo Edmunod Lemus, applied the Mexicana de Aviación logo. Tragically, on 23 April 1979, this jet crashed during a formation take-off from Runway 33 at Ilopango AB while piloted by Teniente Mejia Peña. As usual during the 1970s, instead of a fin flash, it received the national colours over the entire rudder. (Artwork by Luca Canossa)

Founded in 1912 as a rural militia, the Guardia Nacional de El Salvador was a paramilitary force distributed throughout the country's provinces. As of the early 1980s, its uniforms had a ceremonial look and were rather uncomfortable for the climate. They included gloss-black M1 helmets with liner bears and the Army cap badge flanked by 'G' and 'N' (both in gold); a white or light green shirt, with a cotton jacket with metal buttons; tight pants and tall leather leg-warmers ; and this was complemented by a leather suspender belt and magazine pouches. Lettering 'G' and 'N' was also applied on the collars, while the Guardia Nacional's circular emblem was sewn to the left arm. The weaponry of a Guardia Nacional soldier was the (highly popular) German-made, 7.62mm H&K G3 assault rifle. (Artwork by Anderson Subtil)

In the early 1980s, El Salvador began receiving substantial military aid and training from the USA. This resulted in improved equipment and enabled the creation of mobile anti-guerrilla units, like the Rapid Reaction Infantry Battalions (BIRI) and the Rangers (Cazadores). This infantryman of the Cazador Battalion, 3rd Brigade Salvadoran Army – originally trained by Venezuelan advisors, but later by Green Berets of the US Army – is shown as of 1982–1983, while wearing a US-supplied black beret with the 'Cuzcatán' badge (used by this unit at the time), a cotton jacket (probably a left-over from the times of the Vietnam War), and jungle boots. His combat equipment was of the obsolete US 1943 pattern, but his firearm was the relatively modern H&K G3A4 with retractable stock – a standard issue for the Salvadoran Army of the early 1980s. (Artwork by Anderson Subtil)

Renowned for its fierce operations as much as for systematic violations of human rights against the rural population, the Atlacatl was the first of six Rapid Reaction Infantry Battalions (*Batallones de Infanteria de Reacciónmediata*, BIRI) of the Salvadorean Army, trained at Fort Bragg in the USA, by US Special Forces, starting in 1981. In their first counterinsurgency operations, troops of this unit wore fatigues with wavy camouflage pattern of South Korean origin, probably provided by the USA, which used a similar pattern at the time. The rest of their gear was entirely US-made, including the M1 steel helmet, bandoliers for ammunition magazines, canvas belts and jungle boots. The BIRI were the first to be re-equipped with (abundant) US weaponry, including the M16A1 assault rifle calibre 5.56mm, shown here. (Artwork by Anderson Subtil)

This guerrilla girl of the FMLN is shown as seen at the Francisco Sanchez Front, in the Usulután province, in 1983. As of the time, the insurgency could gather around 6,500 to 7,000 'full-time guerrillas' in its regular units, including a plentiful amount of women and teenagers, who were always an important element of the force. Insurgents usually either wore civilian clothes, like this girl, or uniforms stolen from government surplus. The only item with any military appearance was her battered, hand-crafted combat gear. She is shown armed with an M16A1 rifle but the FMLN also had German G3s, Belgian FN FALs, and old US-made M1 Garands. (Artwork by Anderson Subtil)

A map of El Salvador with its provinces. (Map by George Anderson)

to gain the upper hand over the guerrillas. It also prevented new human rights violations which damaged the international image of the government and alienated it from the support of a section of the population.

In February 1981, there were already about 25 American soldiers in El Salvador. The National Security Council approved an additional six-man MTT, bringing the number of Americans to more than 30 who all lived in San Salvador or its immediate vicinity. They were prohibited from taking direct part in combat except in legitimate defence. These soldiers had to assist the FAES in the construction of a military structure capable of successfully confronting an irregular war.[5] The majority were Green Berets but there were also Marine Corps and Air Force members spread across three training centres, one at La Union Naval Base, another at the 5th Infantry Brigade and the last at the FAS Air Base. In March, following an agreement with Congress, the administration increased the number of military advisors to 55 in El Salvador.[6] Besides sending military advisors, Reagan also authorised the first of several large aid shipments to El Salvador. In 1981, Washington granted in total, US$35.4 million of military aid and US$144 million of economic aid.

Salvadoran Army officers trained at the School of the Americas, SOA, in Fort Benning, Georgia, USA. (Albert Grandolini Collection)

The first steps of this counter-insurgency policy took place in a difficult context. Despite the failure of the FMLN offensive, the JRG's position remained fragile. The FAES suffered from several weaknesses and deficiencies as indicated by many US military advisors. According to one of them 'A battalion movement to contact was a single column (line) of some 700 soldiers. Lieutenant Colonels "commanded" these offensive operations from the base tactical operations centre with the AN/PRC-77 radio (17 kilometre range) powered by 110-volt electricity'. Major Cecil Bailey says that 'Maps were scarcer than radio batteries. Artillery forward observers were not attached to brigades and the infantry captains and majors leading in the field did not know how to call for supporting fire'.[7]

Above all, American experts believed that the strategy of the FAES was inappropriate and inconsistent since it conceived the conflict in an awkward way, using an unsuitable 'conventional' approach. This was reflected on the ground by the organisation of major operations mobilising a few thousand soldiers in certain parts of the country. It was then easy for the guerrillas to avoid combat with these forces – who could not play on the surprise – to take refuge in another region before returning when the FAES had withdrawn.

As Ambassador Deane Hinton noted in June 1981, not only was the situation 'bad', but 'things can go against the military'. He added that in the Morazan and Chalatenango departments, two strongholds of the guerrillas, the situation 'is worse today than ever'.[8]

In November 1981, General Fred Woerner was sent to El Salvador to study the FAES. He spent about eight weeks observing them. His findings were overwhelming. The FAES were 'unprepared, strategically, tactically, organisationally, or equipment-wise to confront a credible guerrilla force or insurgency'. According to him,

Salvadoran Army soldiers receive mortar training with a US Advisor. (Albert Grandolini Collection)

the Salvadoran military 'cannot win the war with what they do'. The errors of the FAES were not only military. Woerner showed that the Salvadoran high command did not perceive that Right-wing paramilitary groups were also a threat eroding popular support for the government. For him, it was possible to prevent El Salvador from falling into the hands of the FMLN by massively increasing aid from Washington, in particular by providing weapons and adequate training.[9]

The US military worked to form several aggressive units designed to hunt down and destroy insurgents, the *Batallones de Infantería de Reacción* Inmediata (Immediate Reaction infantry Battalions or BIRI). They were designed to deploy quickly across the country and perform reconnaissance patrols in small units and at long range. The first and most important was the BIRI Atlacatl, which included at its foundation 1,383 soldiers trained in El Salvador by US special forces belonging to the 82nd Airborne Division.[10]

After the creation of the Atlacatl Battalion, two new BIRIs began to form at the end of 1981 with each having 1,000 to 1,200 soldiers; the BIRI Atonal installed at the headquarters of the 4th Infantry Brigade in El Paraiso, Chalatenango, before joining in September 1982 the Usulutan department; the BIRI Belloso installed in the zone of San Bartolo in the north of the capital. These battalions were trained by the American Green Berets, in Panama for the BIRI Atonal and in Fort Bragg, for the BIRI Belloso. BIRI General Manuel José Arce was created in 1983 after training in Honduras. These units obviously received the best equipment available, M-16 rifles, M-60 machine guns and 60 and 80mm mortars.

The seven DMs also saw their numbers increased so that they could each create a Light Infantry Battalion of 700 men. Meanwhile, the Americans formed battalions of Cazadores, 'hunters', after an agreement between El Salvador and Venezuela which sent a team of instructors to organise two of these battalions of 350 men each. The US hoped to build about 14 of these units which, like the BIRIs, were designed to attack the FMLN and perform small-unit, long range reconnaissance missions. However, they operated in a strictly regional framework unlike the BIRIs which could be deployed quickly throughout the country. In 1982, four Cazadores battalions were formed; the Cuscatlan Battalion in the 3rd Infantry Brigade; the Pipil in the 2nd Infantry Brigade; the Jaguar in DM-6; the Sierpe in DM-1, making a total of about 1,400 soldiers.[11]

In addition to the creation of new units intended specifically for the fight against insurgency, Washington was trying to modernise and professionalise those that already existed. The Milgroup decided to increase the numbers of the Airborne squadrons to form a battalion. Their training was carried out in Fort Sherman in Panama and Fort Benning, Georgia. The battalion was officially created on 18 February 1983 with 800 men. It received M-16A1 rifles, M-293 grenade launchers, M-72A2 rocket launchers, M1 and M29 mortars, M40A1 Recoilless Rifles. At the equipment level, at the end of August 1981, Washington sent 4 new UH-1H helicopters to El Salvador, then six others a few months later, giving a total of 20 Bell helicopters supplied during the year 1981.[12]

Another form of American support in El Salvador was the dispatch in February 1982, of the destroyer USS *Deyo*, equipped with a modern electronic spy system, to the Gulf of Fonseca. It was then replaced by the destroyer USS *Caron* which continued its mission in an area where weapons from Nicaragua transited to supply the FMLN.[13]

The policy of the Reagan administration in El Salvador was not without difficulty. The president had to deal with controversy, especially in Congress where the Salvadoran question was a subject of conflict between the executive and legislative powers. On 24

In the territories it controlled, the FMLN installed basic health and public education services to ensure the population's support. (Albert Grandolini Collection)

The Bell UH-1 Iroquois became the biggest and most experienced combat helicopter force in El Salvador, fighting for over a decade and having been trained by US Army in tactics developed during the Vietnam War. In 1981, Washington sent 20 UH-1 to the FAS. (Albert Grandolini Collection)

The support of the population was essential to the FMLN to overcome the failure of the offensive of January 1981. It ensured the logistics of the combatants, provided food, shelter and information. (Albert Grandolini Collection)

September 1981, the Senate decided that aid to El Salvador had to be conditional on the adoption of reforms to enforce human rights and prevent the security forces from committing crimes against the population. Importantly, it ordered the Reagan administration to certify to Congress, improvements in the human rights situation in El Salvador every six months before approving new aid.[14]

The greatest difficulty that the Americans encountered, however, was the reluctance of the FAES to adopt the strategies promoted by their counter-insurgency experts. Despite the massive help from Washington, the latter never managed to have the necessary influence to make the Salvadorans comply with their wishes. The latter were indeed perfectly aware that the White House feared most that El Salvador would become a new Cuba and therefore, placed above all, the maintenance of the Salvadoran government, even at the cost of the rejection by the FAES of certain US advice.

The *Retaguardia*

The failure of the January offensive forced the FMLN to modify its strategy to adapt to a long war. It redefined its objectives and concentrated its efforts mainly on reinforcing the guerrilla structure with weapons and troops trained in Nicaragua or Cuba, which then formed different tactical guerrilla units. The latter had to be concentrated against military objectives from territories called the liberated zone or *retaguardia* (rearguard). This establishment in 1981–1982 drew the contours of a territory that rested on several pockets of dispersed rural insurrections. Public security and State services were no longer guaranteed in these areas where it was now the FMLN squads that assumed control. It an opportunity to establish in these campaigns, a popular power able to provide them with the necessary support to defeat the FAES and conquer the rest of the country.

Relations with the local population were crucial for the FMLN which organised cooperation between combatants and civilians, particularly for agricultural production in order to ensure the supply of food for its troops. For its part, it installed basic health and public education services for the benefit of the population. The *retaguardia* were also organised for the war economy with the installation of arms repair workshops, explosives workshops, production of alcohol for hospitals or fabrics for uniforms and warehouses for food. During military operations, the local population provided information, shelter, supplies and new recruits.[15]

The ERP directed its efforts towards Morazan, the furthest department from San Salvador, essentially the region north of the Torola River, which had only about 30,000 inhabitants at the start of the war. This *retaguardia*, like that of Chalatenango, was of great importance since it bordered with Honduras. The ERP established its power there and formed a logistical and political base which enabled it to develop and concentrate mobile guerrilla battalions. From this zone, it wished to confront the FAES, to extend its territorial control, to make its junction with the other fronts of guerrillas and to end up marching on San Salvador.

In the north of the Chalatenango department, the FPL dominated. As in the Morazan and unlike other *retaguardias*, the pressure from the FAES was less strong there, which offered minimal stability. The FPL organised a logistics base, a military school for officers, a publishing centre for propaganda and particularly, the base of the CG inside El Salvador. This *retaguardia* leaned against neighbouring Honduras and thus benefited from the presence of the refugee camps of San Marcos Ocotepeque.

Apart from the *retaguardia* of Morazan and Chalatenango, the other liberated areas were more precarious. After the January 1981 offensive, a *retaguardia* was created in the east of the Santa Ana department, in the mountains bordering the Lempa River. It was a fragile area, with unstable camps and a weak social base shared by the RN, the ERP and the FPL. In the south of the Usulutan department, the FMLN occupied an important coastal strip, shared between the RN, the FPL, the PRTC and the ERP. On the banks of the Lempa River, the guerrillas controlled the Linares Mountain which commanded both banks of the lower course of the river. This

Guerrilla Forces by Area in 1982[19]	
Morazan	1,000–2,000
La Union	500
Usulutan	700–1,100
Guazapa	1,200
San Vicente	1,000
Chalatenango	1,000–1,500
San Salvador	200
Santa Ana	300

area extended to the Sierra Tecapán Chinameca and Cerro El Tigre, to continue to the bay of Jiquilisco.

Other liberated areas appeared later. In 1981, in reaction to the attack on Sensuntepeque by the guerrillas, the FAES carried out sweeps in the cantons of Santa Marta and San Felipe and around Villa Victoria de Cabañas, forcing the population to take refuge in Honduras. In 1985, RN troops from Chalatenango took control of the depopulated areas of La Cabaña department. The refugees returned in 1987 allowing the FMLN to install its power, to organise production and the population so that they would support it. This newly liberated area served as a communication route along the border with the *retaguardia* of northern Morazan.[16]

Each FMLN organisation had its own *retaguardia*. The FPL dominated in Chalatenango but were also present in the Santa Ana and San Vicente departments. The stronghold of the ERP was Morazan with bases also in Usulutan. Less numerous, the forces of the RN and the PRTC were based in the Cabañas and San Vicente departments but also on the margins of the areas dominated by the ERP and the FPL.[17] There was an exception to this division of the *retaguardias* between organisations, the Cerro de Guazapa, a strategic sector due to its proximity to the capital, where there was a unified command. The latter organised the defence of the territory and worked to control the roads that cross or pass near Guazapa.

The *retaguardias* provided the FMLN with the ability to keep its forces combat-ready and to work with local communities, providing them with social services in return for their support. They were therefore, essential to enable it to overcome the failure of January 1981.[18]

The Battles of Conchagua Volcano and Cerro de Guazapa, February 1981

After the offensive of January 1981, the FAES could rely on their bases in the west of the country and in the main cities, notably San Salvador, to try to eliminate the guerrillas definitively. They launched 28 offensives mobilising more than 1,000 men between February and June 1981. In January, they concentrated on the outskirts of the capital, the sectors of La Vueltas, San Antonio Los Ranchos, Chalchuapa, San Antonio Abad or the volcano of San Salvador.[20]

On a tactical level, the FAES used processes originally designed for conventional warfare and simply transposed them to the fight against guerrillas. Among these tactics was that of *El Yunque y Martin*, the Anvil and the Hammer, which consisted of pushing the enemy towards a predetermined point where the FAES would crush them. A second relied on the encirclement of guerrilla forces, supported by artillery, aviation and helicopters, to tighten the noose on the enemy. The last consisted of saturating a determined area with fire and destroying everything that existed within the delimited perimeter. These different tactics were based on the notion of *tierra arrasada* or scorched earth. For this, civilians were forcibly displaced and those suspected of supporting the FMLN or at least of sympathising with the insurgents, were killed. Terror and population displacement were essentially aimed at depriving the guerrillas of the support of the population.[21]

At the start of the civil war, the tactics employed by the FAES came directly from conventional conflicts. They revolved around the deployment of large numbers of troops concentrated in a specific sector. (Albert Grandolini Collection)

The FAS only used napalm bombs twice, or possibly three times, during the civil war and only during 1981. These bombings were carried out by Ouragan MD-450s. (Albert Grandolini Collection)

One of the first FAES operations took place in the Conchagua volcano, in the south-east of the country, 4km south of La Union. After the January offensive, ERP and FAL forces established defensive positions and encampments there. It was a strategic position that served as a logistics base to receive supplies coming from Nicaragua by sea but also to put pressure on La Union where the DM-3 and the naval base of the Navy were located. It was therefore essential for the FMLN to make this area a solid *retaguardia*.

On 30 January, the guerrillas attacked and seized the small town of Conchagua south of La Union before withdrawing the next day ahead of the arrival of FAES troops. This operation was repeated on 3 February.

Eventually, it attacked La Union. After a few hours of fighting, the rebels end up withdrawing but for the FAES, the guerrillas installed on the volcano represented a permanent threat that had to be destroyed.

The defence of the Conchagua volcano by the ERP was organised in three zones which each had a camp – Plan El Ocotal was the most important. Each had defensive positions but also M-60, BAR, Lewis and M2 machine guns, RPG-2 rocket launchers and M-79 grenade launchers. Lieutenant Colonel Ramon Antonio Morales Ruiz, commander of DM-3, prepared the operation against the Conchagua volcano with a company from the 3rd Infantry Brigade, one from DM-4, one from DM-3, a section of marines and a squadron of paratroopers. This amounted to about 500 men against 300 guerrilla fighters.

The attack began on the morning of 27 February. The paratroopers landed on Zompopero beach and set off north. In a few hours, the access routes to the volcano were held by the FAES. As the military advanced, guerrilla resistance grew stronger. On the evening of the 27th, the FAES spent the night halfway up the volcano. On the morning of the 28th, guerrilla resistance redoubled. An AC-47 aircraft was even hit by a .50 calibre machine gun. The three guerrilla camps were then almost surrounded but the rebels were still resisting on the flat part of the summit of the volcano which they were trying to hold until nightfall in order to be able to withdraw without danger.

On 1st March, FAES forces failed to advance. In the morning, three Ouragan MD-450 each dropped a napalm bomb on the positions still held by the FMLN. It was only the next day that the soldiers resumed their advance and discovered charred bodies. During the night, the guerrillas managed to flee down the ravines to join Jucuaran. After the end of the operation, the FAES set up a military base at the summit of the volcano where the guerrillas could not regain a foothold.[22]

In February 1981, the FAES carried out another clearing operation to dislodge the guerrillas from the Guazapa area. However, the FMLN saw this region as their stronghold which had to be defended no matter the cost. Guazapa was indeed a crucial position to organise and support the urban commandos of San Salvador. For their part, the FAES justified the firepower used by the absence of civilians in the area, which was false. However, they had to recognise that the situation in this region was difficult, as they were encountering strong resistance. One of the fiercest battles was taking place on the hill of Guazapa, where the guerrillas were said to have gathered around 500 fighters. The FAES operation ended on 6 April 1981 with the only success being the takeover of its summit. The guerrillas remained firmly established in the rest of Cerro de Guazapa.[23]

The FAES also carried out operations in the San Vicente and Zacatecoluca departments whilst the 1st Infantry Brigade destroyed an FMLN camp in Cerro La Ventanas near El Paisnal at the end of February.

The Battle of La Guacamaya, March 1981

After the January offensive, Villalobos, the leader of the ERP, gathered his forces – between 400 and 500 fighters – in northern Morazan, particularly in La Guacamaya sector. It was an excellent defensive position, covered with abundant vegetation and surrounded by low heights that provided points of observation and defence. Here were located the ERP General Staff, the Radio Venceremos Station which began broadcasting on 12 January 1981, a small hospital and propaganda structures. Its defence consisted of anti-aircraft trenches and shelters built for the occupants of the camp. In the vicinity were six other camps which formed a wider defensive perimeter. The ERP demonstrated its willingness to fight the FAES in a conventional positional war.

The BIRI Atlacatl was the most famous counter-insurgency unit of the FAES. It took part in almost all the major operations carried out against the FMLN. (Albert Grandolini Collection)

On 2 March, two ERP platoons commanded by Commander William Antonio Pascasio attacked the small garrison of Meanguera. The soldiers resisted, but they had eight dead. This action was part of the campaign of the ERP to destroy the small military detachments north of the Torola River in order to expand and consolidate its *retaguardia*. To ward off this threat, the FAES decided to organise a major operation whose objective was to destroy the command of the ERP, the Radio Venceremos Station and more broadly to eradicate the presence of the FMLN in the north of Morazan. When the ERP leadership became aware of FAES offensive preparations, it accelerated the construction of defensive positions.

The FAES mobilised around 1,600 soldiers from two Commando companies, a squadron of paratroopers, a company from the 5th Infantry Brigade, the 1st company from the BIRI Atlacatl and an artillery battery. These forces appeared modest but their armament was far superior to that of the guerrillas. Above all, they could rely on 700 members of the security forces or the Civil Defence whilst the guerrillas had only about 500 fighters.

The operation began on 10 March and the first battles opposed the guerrillas to the paratroopers in the Agua Blanca sector. The latter managed to reach Las Lomas the next day, then on the 12th, the Joateca volcano, near La Gacayama, where they encountered strong resistance. The support of a battery of 120mm mortars did not allow them to progress. On 13 March, the BIRI Atlacatl reached the north of Perquin before advancing east without encountering resistance. On the 16th and 17th, it seized Arambala north of La Guacayama, dangerously threatening the guerrillas, especially their positions near El Mozote.[24] During these days, the FAES committed abuses against the civilian population such as the massacre of El Junquillo where 70 civilians were executed by the DM-6 of Sonsonate.[25]

On 19 March, the paratroopers reached the Sapo River and approached the ERP command post. The BIRI Atlacatl continued to advance south from Arambala but two platoons were ambushed. The soldiers managed to retreat but the guerrillas prevented the manoeuvrer to envelop their defensive positions. DM-3 forces were then sent by helicopter to the Arambala area to prevent the BIRI Atlacatl from collapsing.

For his part, Villalobos asked to organise a defence in the Cerro Los Marquez to prevent the crossing of the Sapo River by the paratroopers. For this, the ERP sent a reinforcement of 25 fighters whilst three defensive lines were formed, each consisting of two trenches connected to each other. The first line of defence, near the Sapo River was defended by 13 men, the second by 12 and the last, on the ridge, by 25. The first line resisted until 22 March. Guerrilla resistance was fierce.

A FAES soldier in combat in the Chalatenango department. (Albert Grandolini Collection)

On the 23rd, a parachute squadron arrived as reinforcements to tighten the noose around La Guacayama. But it was blocked by the guerrillas in the Cerro El Tablon. To break the resistance of the ERP, the paratroopers requested the intervention of the FAS. Two Ouragans fighters, each armed with two napalm bombs, went into action. Of the four bombs, one did not explode. This bombardment on La Guacayama and that of the artillery on El Tablon weakened the defences of the FMLN allowing the paratroopers to seize El Tablon. The next day, three Ouragans bombarded the Cerro Gate de Monte, this time with bombs without napalm. On the 24th, Fouga Magisters and Ouragans bombed La Guacamaya, also under fire from 81mm mortar batteries before the paratroopers launched new assaults that the guerrillas always managed to repel.

On the 25th, in a new manoeuvrer launched from Arambala, BIRI Atlacatl soldiers managed to infiltrate the guerrilla positions in El Mozote with the support of DM-3 troops. They received air support from an Arava but again guerrilla resistance was strong and the military had to withdraw. On the 26th, the ERP second line of defence on the Sapo River fell under the constant assaults of the FAES.[26] On the 28th, the soldiers even managed to locate the Radio Venceremos Station. Two Fougas bombarded it and then machine-gunned the area but the shelter built to protect the radio station resisted the explosions.[27]

The situation of the guerrillas became desperate, the ammunition began to run out and some commanders criticised the decision taken to defend fixed positions against the firepower of the military. On the 29th, the FAS again bombarded the positions of the FMLN whilst the troops of the DM-3 and BIRI Atlacatl, advanced again on El Mozote. The weak guerrilla forces nevertheless managed to check their advance, allowing the ERP to withdraw all of its forces on the night of 30 March.[28]

According to estimates, the fighting caused the death of around 30 guerrillas and 14 soldiers. This victory of the FAES caused optimism within the government. Nevertheless, the guerrillas managed to escape destruction after 26 days of valiant combat, withstanding a vastly superior opponent. Above all, once the soldiers left the area, the FMLN returned and settled in Cerro Zapotal, just 3km from La Guacayama.

The FAES had more difficulty in the Cerro de Guazapa in April. More than 3,000 soldiers surrounded the area which was bombarded by Fouga Magisters. The infantry went on the attack by climbing the slopes of the volcano. The guerrillas responded by launching groups of five fighters to hit the rear and flanks of the FAES columns. Finally, the soldiers withdrew to their starting base after having lost 150 men against eight from the FMLN.[29]

Fighting in Morazan and Chalatenango, August–December 1981

Across the country, the FAES launched search and destroy operations in order to drive the FMLN out of populated areas, push them back into the mountains and concentrate the firepower of the FAS and the artillery on their forces. In northern Morazan department, the guerrilla columns retreated west of Jocaitique whilst the FAES launched an operation from northern San Miguel towards San Diego south-west of Torola, pushing the guerrillas towards El Zapotal to the north of Jocoaitique. Only the rainy season put an end to the advance of the military.[30] In Chalatenango department, the BIRI Belloso went into action in June 1981 and together with the BIRI Atlacatl, participated in a scorched earth operation with the support of artillery and aviation, in the mountains of La Cañada, Chupamiel, Los Filos and El Portillo which border Honduras. This operation resulted in the flight of many inhabitants to refuges in Honduras.[31]

These successes made the FAES believe that they were close to victory. They managed to set up permanent bases in sectors hitherto held by the guerrillas, to reinforce the security forces scattered in these regions and to install Civil Defence forces there. This optimism soon collided with the directives of the FMLN CG which asked each organisation to form mobile units capable of besieging and destroying military posts, especially the most isolated and the most difficult to reinforce.[32]

In early April 1981, the concentration of guerrilla forces in northern Morazan continued. Thus, Commander Claudio Armijo's column arrived from the south-eastern front and on 16 April, attacked Villa del Rosario, north-east of San Isidro. In reaction, on the 22nd, the Commandos based in San Francisco Gotera tried to cross the Torola River but it was not until 1 May that the guerrillas were pushed back towards the canton of Zapotal.[33] The

The small posts and garrisons of the security forces (here GN members) were particularly vulnerable to guerrilla attacks. (Albert Grandolini Collection)

The mountains surrounding Perquin were the refuge of hundreds of ERP fighters. In June, the control of the guerrillas over the region was increasingly strong and the patrols of the FAES could no longer move away from their bases where they were practically besieged. Perquin was a small town of only 1,500 inhabitants but it was at the crossroads of the roads leading to the north of Morazan. For the FAES, its loss would mean the impossibility of organising resistance in the region and would allow the guerrillas to control the north of the department between the Torola River and the border.

In the city there was a GN post reinforced by a section of Commandos and members of the Civil Defence. Around Perquin, in La Guacamaya, there was a Commando company; in Torola, a PH post reinforced by a group of Civil Defence and in Osicala, a GN and Civil Defence post. These dispersed forces were the victims of constant harassment. To stop this, in July 1981, Lieutenant Colonel José Alejandro Cisneros, commander of CICFA, prepared an offensive which was to lead the FAES to the border with Honduras. For its part, the ERP was preparing to conquer all the military posts north of the Torola River, starting with Perquin.

The Mazinger, the armoured and armed civilian trucks used by the FAES, were particularly vulnerable to RPG fire from the guerrillas. In this picture, a MAN-based Mazinger with triple 20mm cannon, a pair of 90mm recoilless rifles and light machine gun mounts. (Albert Grandolini Collection)

ERP continued its actions of harassment in the region, particularly in Perquin, Jocoaitique and La Guacamaya. The tactic was simple, a unit attacked a small outpost of the FAES whilst other forces organised an ambush against the troops coming to rescue the attacked soldiers. Another tactic was to engage in combat only after getting as close as possible to the soldiers so that they could not take advantage of their firepower.[34]

The arrival of new weapons by air and sea allowed the guerrillas to recover their firepower whilst measures were taken to improve the coordination of their various forces. This enabled the FMLN on 19 July, to launch its first offensive since that of January, in order to contest the initiative of the FAES. The offensive lasted until August and resulted in important battles such as the capture of Perquin.

The mission given to Jorge Antonio Meléndez, commander of the ERP forces in northern Morazan, was to attack Perquin and then reunite with other ERP troops to attack San Fernando, Torola, Meanguera and Jocoaitique. The objective was to reach the banks of the Torola River to build new defensive positions there. Against Perquin, ERP had three columns, led by commanders Gregorio Portillo Martinez, Maximiliano Vasquez Vigil and Walter de Jesus Argueta Rodriguez, which represented about 300 men including the forces used to build roadblocks.[35]

On the morning of the 10th, Portillo's column attacked Perquin from the south whilst that of Maximiliano Vasquez advanced from the north and north-east and that of Walter de Jesus Argueta also advanced from the north. Elsewhere, ERP forces attacked FAES or security force positions in San Fernando, Torola, San Simon, Meanguera and Jocoaitique. Perquin was only defended by 22 members of the GN and 20 of the Civil Defence who quickly found themselves besieged but managed to resist.[36] They asked for help from the FAS, which sent two Ouragan fighter-bombers to drop four bombs on the guerrilla positions and then machine-gunned them.[37] They were joined by two UH-1H helicopters which used their machine guns. The rebels on their side installed machine guns of .50 calibre on heights whose shots prevented the helicopters from manoeuvring. Finally, on the 12th and after 48 hours of combat, the garrison of Perquin surrendered.

When the attack on Perquin was announced, Lieutenant Colonel Cisneros decided to send a Commando section which left La Guacamaya in the direction of El Mozote to join Perquin from the south-east. It passed through El Mozote without being spotted by the guerrillas. When the latter realised it mistake, it began the pursuit of the soldiers. A skirmish broke out but part of the rebel forces managed to reach the top of Cerro de Arambala and blocked the advance of the soldiers[38]. On the morning of the 11th, the guerrillas received reinforcements and organised an ambush for the Commandos who were defeated, only nine soldiers managing to flee.[39]

At the same time, another section of Commandos was transported by helicopter to the north-east of Perquin to support the 2nd company of Commandos coming from Meanguera accompanied by a Mazinger, a Magiruz truck equipped with an anti-aircraft gun of 20mm, and a power truck armed with a Browning .30 machine gun. Due to delays, the column did not leave until the 14th. It crossed the Torola River and fell into an ambush south of Jocoaitique organised by ERP forces, commanded by Angel Patojo. After a few hours of fighting, the soldiers had to retreat to Meanguera.

Faced with the failures of these troops, the FAES General Staff decided to send the paratroopers to recapture Perquin. These were reinforced by 140 soldiers from the DM-6. On the 17th, the paratroopers were transported to San Fernando, which was only 3km from Perquin. They progressed to the north of the locality which they prepared to attack on the morning of 18 August.

At 6:00 a.m., a C-47 machine-gunned the guerrilla positions at Perquin, but due to the fog, its action had no effect. For their part, the paratroopers went on the attack, surprising the ERP forces which quickly broke up. At 7:00 a.m., with the soldiers of DM-6, they completely controlled Perquin and its surroundings. On the 19th, whilst patrolling the region to flush out the rebel forces, the paratroopers discovered a concentration of 200 guerrillas. Despite the firepower of the FAES, the guerrillas firmly resisted, forcing the soldiers to return to Perquin. On the way back, they were intercepted by ERP troops who managed to surround them despite the support of SOCATA Rallye 235GT aircraft equipped with Matra RL F2 rockets. Only the arrival of the soldiers of the DM-6, which forced the guerrillas to withdraw, allowed the paratroopers not to succumb. ERP forces eventually retreated north of Torola, west of Perquin and south-west of Joateca.[40]

On 12 August, at the same time as the guerrillas seized Perquin in Morazan, they also captured San José Guayabal, in the Cuscatlan department, destroying its garrison. The FMLN also increased ambushes on the Pan-American and Litoral Highways and managed to place two explosive charges in the PN garrison in San Salvador which was half destroyed.[41] In response, from 9 to 15 September, the FAES mobilised 1,800 soldiers from the DMs of Ahuachapan, Usulutan and La Union, as well as from the BIRI Atlacatl, for an operation in Morazan.

In Chalatenango, a region where the FPL were firmly established, the guerrillas, as in Morazan, attacked the garrisons in the north of the department. This situation pushed the FAES to install the

Left-wing guerrillas from the FPL posed with their rifles in Santa Anita, Chalatenango department. (Albert Grandolini Collection)

new BIRI Atonal in El Paraiso in the buildings of the 4th Infantry Brigade. The FAES General Staff also decided to launch a major offensive to destroy the guerrillas in this region. The objective was the region of Ojos de Agua, at the north-east end of the department which bordered the Sumpul River which marked the border with Honduras and where there were about 10 villages held by the FMLN.

The strategy used for this operation was again that of the Hammer and the Anvil carried out by 'Hybrid Battalions', which was formed by infantry companies from different garrisons. The first included a DM-6 company, a foot cavalry squadron and an Airborne squadron. It had to form the Anvil going from the township of El Jicaro to the township of Yurique. Another Battalion made up of two companies of the 4th Infantry Brigade and a company of DM-1 advanced from the south. The Hammer was made up of three companies of the BIRI Atlacatl which advanced from the north from the Volcancillo sector. Further south, in the Cabañas department, other FAES forces were searching for guerrilla camps in the areas of Suchitoto, Cinquera, Tejutepeque and Jutiapa. The operation mobilised around 7,000 soldiers.

It began on 30 September with the landing of paratroopers around Ojo de Agua. They did not meet resistance, which was not the case for units coming from the south, like that of the DM-1 which faced hard guerrillas. The soldiers did not know that a meeting of the leadership of the FPL was being held in the sector in the presence of Carpio, who was evacuated. Finally, on 6 October, the FPL forces stormed the positions held by the DM-6 and opened a path north, towards the Sumpul River, thus escaping the encirclement.[42]

In October, the FAES attacked Jucuaran, in the south of the Usulutan department, then from 2 to 5 November, the Chinchontepec volcano in the department of San Vicente, using mainly artillery and aviation. From 9 to 16 November, and then from 18 to 26 November, FAES operations took place in the department of La Cabaña. On this occasion, the soldiers even entered the territory of Honduras in order to strike at the rear of the FMLN.[43]

The UH-1H helicopters proved to be essential during the FAES counterinsurgency operations. (Albert Grandolini Collection)

The FAES were also preparing a new operation in Morazan department. During its preparation, General Garcia declared: 'With this operation we will take away the FMLN's offensive capabilities. We'll try to kill off their forces and diminish their supply of ammunition and finally, we will apply enough pressure to cut their supply lines'. For his part, Colonel Castillo announced 'Advancing on the enemy should be done through penetrative surprise assaults. We must push forward without stopping for any reason, regardless of the circumstances. We must reach their command post and Radio Venceremos. Domingo [Monterrosa], you and your Atlacatl Battalion will really have to show your stuff'.[44]

From 7 to 29 December, the FAES concentrated in northern Morazan from 4,000 to 5,000 men for Operation Rescate. Among the troops participating were the BIRI Atlacatl, units of the 3rd Infantry Brigade and Commandos from San Francisco Gotera. The strategy was not original, it was always that of the Hammer, in that this operation came from the north, and the Anvil, installed in the south. The operation began with aerial bombardments, particularly in the canton La Joya. The BIRI Atlacatl landed by helicopter at Perquin and were deployed whilst the other forces came from San Francisco Gotera. The operation had little success as the FMLN avoided being caught between the Hammer and the Anvil and its troops managed to easily break the encirclement.

As the FAES scoured the countryside, they often harassed or terrorised villagers, sometimes destroying entire villages. This happened in El Mozote where the BIRI Atlacatl rounded up and murdered hundreds of civilians on 11 December. The number of victims was controversial. The UN Truth Commission put it at 'more than 200'. A list compiled by Tutela Legal, the human rights office of the Archdiocese of San Salvador, said 767 people have died.[45] In the following days, massacres were still committed in Rancherias, Los Toriles, La Joya, Poza Honda, El Rincon, El Potrero, Yancolo, Flor de Muerto and Pando Hill.

Operation Rescate ultimately ended in defeat for the FAES. On 29 December, a reinforced column comprising between 150 and 200 fighters, commanded by Angel Patojo, received the order to attack the military positions in La Guacamaya held by a company of the 3rd Infantry Brigade. The fighting lasted all day and despite the fire from the 105mm howitzers based in Osicala, the noose tightened on the soldiers who were defeated. The lieutenant who commanded them committed suicide so as not to be taken prisoner and only a few survivors managed to reach Osicala.

During 1981, most of the fighting took place in the Chalatenango, Cabañas, San Vicente, Usulutan, Morazan departments and in the Guazapa area near San Salvador. The FMLN, installed in its *retaguardias* of Chalatenango and Morazan, exploited the need for the FAES to maintain its control over the whole country. It did this by installing small garrisons which proved vulnerable whilst the reinforcements sent to defend them were victims of ambushes. Thus, the guerrillas consolidated their territorial presence and could gain combat experience before facing larger military units in the open. The FAES offensives which sought to fix the positions of the FMLN and then launched violent blows against them using large contingents of troops, proved to be ineffective and exhausted their limited resources.[46]

The FAES failures to destroy the FMLN served to galvanise the morale of the guerrillas. This new state of mind, the arrival of new weapons and new fighters, the increase in the number of cadres trained abroad and the experience of real combat, pushed the leadership of the FMLN to want to organise regional offensives. They had to exhaust the FAES and demonstrate that the guerrillas were an effective force, capable, if the circumstances were favourable, of winning a strategic victory.

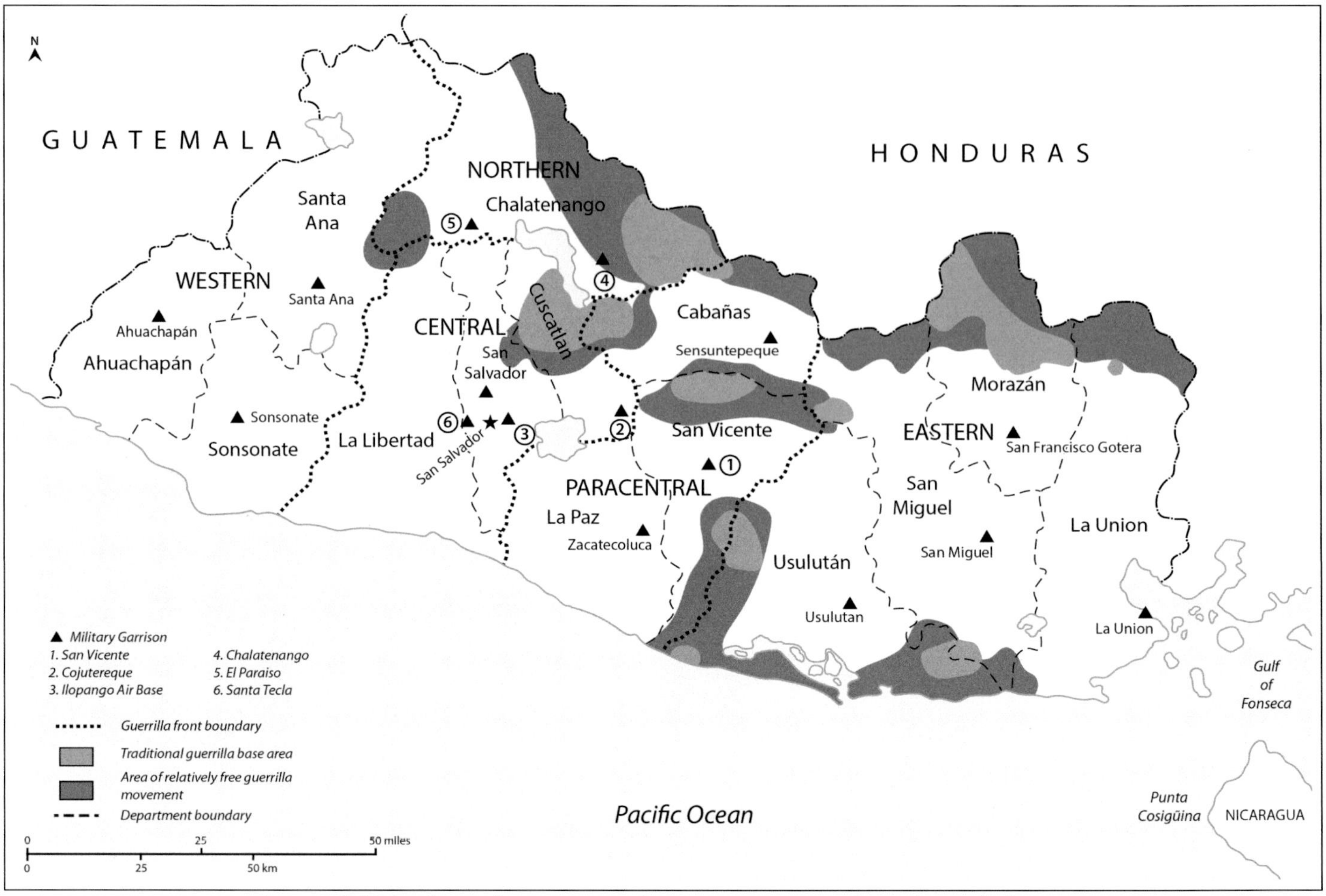

A map of El Salvador as of 1981-1982, with areas containing traditional guerrilla bases and their relatively free movement. (Map by George Anderson)

6

THE GUERRILLAS TOOK THE INITIATIVE

During the first months of the war, the FMLN discovered that it was in a better position than it had been before the January 1981 offensive. Whilst the FAES won tactical victories, they spent their resources and although the United States agreed to provide military aid, the reluctance of the US Congress meant that this would not arrive quickly. The FMLN considered that this delay could be

The FMLN's sabotage campaigns aimed both to increase public discontent against the government and to weaken the economy. The destruction of electricity pylons which deprived part of the country of electricity, was particularly effective in achieving these objectives. (Albert Grandolini Collection)

favourable for it to gain the upper hand over the FAES and weaken the Salvadoran government.

FAES soldiers under fire. (Albert Grandolini Collection)

The FMLN Sabotage Campaign

Since mid-1981, the main elements of the FMLN's strategy had evolved to adapt those of a protracted people's war. In addition to the establishment of *retaguardias*, it highlighted the destruction of national infrastructure and the demoralisation of the FAES. Against the military this resulted in the tactic of *el desgaste* or attrition, which was based on surprise attacks, ambushes with small patrols, the use of artisanal mines and the capture of small localities. This tactic was effective since the Woerner Report noted that 75 percent of military casualties were the 'result of ambushes (mainly vehicles) and mines or booby traps'.[1] At the end of 1981, the FAES lost 3,827 men, dead, wounded or missing, which represented 19 percent of these forces. This high level of casualty, combined with the FMLN policy of releasing captured soldiers, eroded the will to fight of many poorly trained units where soldier morale was low.[2]

Regarding the destruction of infrastructure, from the summer of 1981, the FMLN launched a coordinated campaign of sabotage against the electricity network by destroying 59 electricity pylons. Roads were cut and bridges destroyed such as the one at Puente de Oro on 15 October 1981, cutting the country in two. This latter operation was carried out by a team of FPL special forces, accompanied by some Cubans whilst about 500 guerrillas attacked the soldiers of the DM-4 and the PH who were defending the bridge.[3]

These sabotage campaigns served several purposes. Firstly, it impeded the functioning of the economy, which in turn increased the discontent of the population. Secondly, they were a means of demonstrating the government's inability to protect the population. Militarily, sabotage forced the FAES to disperse its forces into small units to protect the infrastructure, offering the FMLN the possibility of concentrating its units in order to be able to strike them.

This strategy was effective. The US Department of State estimated that FMLN caused US$826 million in damage to the Salvadoran economy between 1979 and 1983 whilst the total cumulative economic aid from the United States during this period is US$607 million. These attacks continued throughout the conflict, straining the resources of the Salvadoran authorities. Not only did the FMLN strategy prevent economic growth but it kept the government dependent on US aid.[4]

Battles in the Morazan, January 1982

At the beginning of 1982, the FMLN launched actions not only in Morazan but also in the Chalatenango, San Vicente and Usulatan departments. In Morazan department, where the ERP – after its victory of La Guacamaya on 29 December 1981 – had about 900 men, the main targets were Jocoaitique, San Isidro and Corinto.

Jocoaitique was a small town of a thousand inhabitants 50km north of San Francisco Gotera, halfway between Perquin and Meanguera. It was defended by 26 soldiers who had installed defensive positions on a height, La Planta, 600m north of the city but also by 20 GN and 40 members of the Civil Defence. The operation against Jocoaitique was led by Silvio de Jesus Argueta alias Licho who installed, opposite La Planta, the forces of Commander José Ismael Romero Hernandez alias Bracamonte, responsible for both intercepting the troops coming from the north and fixing the soldiers in their positions. In addition to the Bracamonte forces, the ERP mobilised two columns led by Maximiliano Vasquez Vigil alias Goyo Negro, and Walter de Jesus Argueta Rodriguez alias Che Guevara, as well as in effect, about 260 to 300 men.

FES fighters, under the orders of Leonidas Monteagudo Hernandez alias Guadalupe, infiltrated the enemy defences on the morning of 12 January 1982 and attacked the GN barracks with two RPG-2s, giving the signal for the start of the attack. The FAS quickly sent Fouga to bombard the positions of the guerrillas and the helicopters which strafed them. In the city, the fights were violent but by the end of the afternoon, the ERP completely controlled it. The soldiers installed in La Planta tried to rescue Jocoaitique but they were held back by the forces of Bracamonte.[5] GN reinforcements were also landed by helicopters 2km from the city, but they were repulsed and had to withdraw to Meanguera.[6]

Corinto was the next ERP target. It was a small town that connected the Morazan department to the north with that of La Union. Above all, it allowed the FAES to attack the FMLN positions north of Morazan from the east and had a garrison of 20 Civil Defence members, reinforced by a PH post of 20 agents. On 31 January, the guerrillas attacked Corinto and after heavy fighting, the resistance ceased, the head of the Civil Defence was captured and taken to the Zapotal camp where he was summarily executed.

The FAES staff decided to recapture Corinto by an airborne operation. The commander of the paratroopers deemed it necessary to make a jump as close as possible to the city in order to take the enemy by surprise. The operation mobilised 144 paratroopers. On 1st February, the latter jumped east of the city from four C-47s.

During the FMLN attack on Ilopango Air Base, the FAS lost 75 percent of their aircraft, including four C-47s like this armed example. (Albert Grandolini Collection)

They regrouped to advance on Corinto and surrounded it. The fight began against about 200 guerrillas and lasted nearly eight hours. The guerrilla resistance was so fierce that the encirclement of the city was not complete, which finally allowed it to withdraw at dusk.[7] At the end of the fighting, the soldiers announced that they had 10 wounded and no dead, whilst the FMLN left 15 dead on the ground and took the others away.

The Attack on Ilopango Air Base, February 1982

Since the offensive of January 1981, the management of the ERP had wanted to strike a blow to the FAES which would have both a major national echo and which did not require the mobilisation of a large force. The chosen target was the FAS base in Ilopango. In April 1981, Villalobos asked the leader of the Central Front, Arquimides Antonio Cañada alias Alejandro Montenegro, to select eight of the best urban guerrilla fighters of the ERP to receive an intensive 45-day training at the Special Forces School of Matanzas in Cuba. Thanks to photographs of Ilopango, taken from small planes of the FMLN, the Cubans even built a replica of the base.[8]

In October 1981, Montenegro reunited with Villalobos in Managua. The latter told him that the commando was ready, and it could act. During the months of November and December, the men of the commando carried out reconnaissance of the base, finalising the plan of the operation and choosing the routes of infiltration and retreat with the help of two soldiers who were members of the FMLN. They decided to go on the attack on 27 February when the fighting at Jocoaitique and Corinto the previous month had showed that the FAS was a serious threat to the guerrillas. The time had come to deal it a severe blow, even to paralyse it.

On the evening of the 26th, the ERP commando moved into its starting positions. It entered the base through the south-west sector of the airstrip. After an hour of progress, it laid explosive charges and managed to withdraw without being detected, before being evacuated by civilian vehicles. At 2:10 a.m. on the 27th, the explosions began. FAS defence teams sprang into action, believing the base was under attack. Two UH-1H helicopters took off in an emergency, one even machine-gunned an area where it thought the attackers were. In a security house in the Satélite Colonia, Montenegro heard the explosions. The mission was a success, 17 UH-1H helicopters, seven Ouragan fighter-bombers and four C-47s were destroyed or damaged, which represented 75 percent of the FAS aircraft.[9]

The 1982 Elections

It became clear at the start of 1982 that the war would be long. This required the Salvadoran and American governments to put in place a far-reaching political and military strategy. On the military level, in the first days of February 1982, Reagan authorised US$55 million military aid to El Salvador. Washington would thus provide US$82 million for the year 1982. On 6 February, the Americans also delivered six UH-1H helicopters then two others in August.[10] Politically, the Reagan Administration and the JRG wanted to create institutions that appeared legitimate to the population. In this perspective, the organisation of elections allowing the formation of a moderate political Centre against the extreme Left and Right, was considered essential. The goal was to replace the military regime with a civilian government capable of gaining support at home and abroad. Elections were also a way for the Reagan Administration to gain congressional support to continue funding the war against the FMLN.

It was still reeling from the attack on the Ilopango base when the first elections planned by the JRG were organised – those for the designation of the Constituent Assembly on 28 March 1982. Despite the desire to ensure by these means, the popular and international legitimacy of Salvadoran power, the electoral process excluded the FMLN, as well as Left-wing parties such as the FDR whose security was not guaranteed against the death squads but above all, because the FAES refused the participation of Left-wing parties in the elections

Which attitude to adopt towards these elections provoked debates within the FMLN. For the ERP and the RN, it was necessary to cause their boycott in at least 80 percent of the municipalities and to seize garrisons in the big cities. With Cuban support, the ERP suggested a return to the insurrectionary strategy by proposing to capture the Usulutan garrison and to harass those of San Miguel and San Francisco Gotera. Vilallobos offered a strategic battle that

A soldier steps out of a tailor's workshop during a battle between the army and guerrilla units in Cuscatancingo, a suburb of San Salvador during the March 1982 elections. (Albert Grandolini Collection)

The capture of Usulutan in March 1982, which the FMLN held for a week, demonstrated the progress made by the guerrillas since the January 1981 offensive. (Albert Grandolini Collection)

would mobilise all the forces of the FMLN and could provoke the insurrection.

Carpio opposed these proposals, deemed 'petty-bourgeois', incapable of leading to a military or negotiated solution to the conflict. He believed as in January 1981, the insurrection would not be there and preferred that the FMLN confined itself to limited actions against the outskirts of the cities. He refused what he thought was a waste of effort and resources.[11] Nevertheless, Villalobos obtained the power to launch an operation against Usulutan with the hope that this choice validated the maintenance of its insurrectional strategic option.

As the elections approached, the FMLN proclaimed that the population had to prepare for an imminent insurrection and the FAES decided to destroy its camps in the Jucuaran region. The offensive which began on 6 February, brought together around 2,600 soldiers. Forces of the 1st and 3rd Infantry Brigades, DM-1, 3 and 4, BIRI Atlacatl advanced from north to south and encountered concentrations of guerrillas at Los Desmontes, Hacienda San Pedro, Mejicapa and especially around Jucuaran. The resistance of the guerrillas, which gathered in this sector about 600 men, was so strong that it forced the FAES to use 105mm guns and 81mm mortars for two days. On 13 February, the FAES forces split into three groups in order to corner the guerrillas against the Grande River. In the sectors of Cerro El Mono and El Monito, south of Jucuaran, camps were destroyed and the soldiers set up small detachments in Jucuaran and in the villages in the area, to prevent the movements of the guerrillas.[12] Nevertheless, the military operation did not hinder the military preparations of the FMLN for the elections. The guerrillas thus carried out raids on San Miguel, Santa Ana and San Vicente on 8 March.[13]

Usulutan, located 100km south-east of San Salvador, had 40,000 inhabitants and dominated in a rich region, due to the cultivation of coffee, which was important in this department. The city, the main objective of the FMLN for the March elections, was defended by the DM-4, commanded by Lieutenant Colonel Elmer Gonzalez Araujo, whose units occupied defensive positions in the localities of the department and defended the air strip of the Hacienda La Carrera, 8km west of Usulutan. In the port of El Triunfo and in the bay of Jiquilisco there was a base of the National Navy with 20 to 30 sailors. In addition to these numbers, there were the garrisons of the GN and the PN. However, in the town of Usulutan, there were only 448 military and 40 security forces present, reinforced since mid-1981 by two Mazinger and Astroboy armoured vehicles and a jeep Ford Mutt armed with a 12.7mm machine gun.[14] This weakness of the garrison was one of the elements which determined the choice of the FMLN.

The command of the DM-4 realised that the guerrillas were preparing a major operation. On 25 March, it sent units to carry out offensive actions in the north-east and east of Usulutan where they clashed with guerrilla forces. In response, the latter attacked the small garrison of Puerto Parada, killing five soldiers and wounding two members of the Civil Defence.

For the attack against Usulutan, Commander Balta had 590 fighters, 200 of whom belong to the ERP. The FAL mobilised 40 men, the FPL a Vanguard Units column with 130 men, the FARN 40 men and the FAR-LP 80 men. Added to this were a hundred ERP militiamen. The objective of the operation was to stay in the city, to besiege the garrison until the population raised in insurrection and allowed it to be taken under control.

On the morning of the 28 March, the guerrilla forces managed to quickly overrun the FAES positions, which nevertheless, avoided being surrounded and withdrew to other positions. The guerrillas reached the centre of the city and thanks to the firing of three anti-tank rockets, they even opened a breach in the wall of the DM-4 barracks but without managing to invest it.

To support the Usulutan garrison, an Airborne squadron left Ilopango and landed in the early afternoon on the small airstrip of Hacienda La Carrera then advanced towards the city. It was joined in the evening by units of BIRI Atlacatl and Belloso to attack in the southwestern sector of the city. The next day, the fighting was

Salvadoran Army troops advance on guerrilla positions in a poor neighbourhood of the capital in March 1982 (Albert Grandolini Collection)

violent in the outskirts of Usulutan and the FAES troops needed the support of the FAS. A Lama and a UH-1H entered the battle, bombarding and strafing the guerrilla positions. The paratroopers managed to reach the main entrance of Usulatan where they again faced strong resistance. They were joined by agents of the PN whose barracks were close and especially by a Mazinger.

On the evening of the 29th, the troops of the DM-4 and the security forces were still on the defensive in the city, contented to repel the attacks. Only the paratroopers put pressure on the positions of the FMLN west of the city. Faced with the lack of popular participation in the fighting, the guerrillas concentrated their efforts against the FAES. On the 30th, they attacked the PN barracks with grenade launchers and RPG-2s which succeeded in destroying the front door. The DM-4 had to send reinforcements and the Mazinger whilst the paratroopers were still blocked west of the city. Only the arrival of these reinforcements prevented the police from having to flee. Another guerrilla force advanced from the south and blocked the BIRI Atlacatl and Atonal.

Time was nevertheless playing against the FMLN since new FAES reinforcements were approaching the city. On 30 March, two infantry companies of the 3rd Infantry Brigade arrived east of Usulutan along with the rest of the BIRI Atlacatl. These reinforcements were to launch a counter-attack on 1st April to the south and south-east whilst the DM-4 forces would advance west. New reinforcements from the 3rd Infantry Brigades, DM-6 and 7 had to attack towards the north and north-east. The objective was to surround the guerrilla units besieging the garrison.

On 1 April, the FAES went on the attack against the guerrilla fortifications and barricades whilst Huey helicopters spotted their positions and machine-gunned them. At El Ojushte, part of the DM-6 forces organised an ambush against guerrilla troops trying to escape the encirclement whilst the other part jostled the rebel forces who were still attacking the garrison of the DM-4. The units of the 3rd Infantry Brigade also prevailed over the retreating guerrillas. In Usulutan, remnants of DM-4 and paratroopers secured the town.

On 2 April, Comandante Gonzalo attempted a daring manoeuvrer. He took advantage of the weak defence of the south-eastern access of Usulutan to advance with a small force to its centre. He had to nevertheless, face the troops of the BIRI Atlacatl in violent combats where he ended up finding his death. The loss of Gonzalo demoralised his forces which no longer resisted the attacks of the militaries.

During the night, Balta finally decided to evacuate the area. He divided his forces into two groups, one headed north towards the Usulutan volcano and the other went south to reach the Jucuaran area. During the operation against Usulatan, the losses of the guerrillas would have been about 100 combatants whilst the FAES had 32 dead and 70 wounded. About 30 civilians also lost their lives in the fighting in the city[15]. For the first time since the beginning of the civil war, the guerrillas managed to keep control of a large city for a week.

In the rest of the country, the FAL and the FAR-LP refused to attack San Vicente. Elsewhere, fighting was taking place in the cities of Santa Ana, San Miguel, San Francisco Gotera, Zacatecoluca and also in San Salvador. In San Francisco Gotera, the guerrillas held the peaks that dominated the city, seized the airstrip and threatened the hospital. They were repelled by BIRI Atlacatl forces supported by an APC armed with a .50-calibre machine gun and a UH-1 helicopter. In Chalatenango, the guerrillas attacked the capital of the department but also the electricity dam of Cerron Grande. They blocked traffic on the Litoral Highway by destroying a bridge between San Marcos Lempa and El Castano. It was in this department that on 17 March, five Dutch journalists accompanying FMLN fighters were killed in an ambush organised by the BIRI Atonal.[16]

Whilst the government concentrated many troops in San Salvador, the FMLN sought to enter the capital on the night of 27 to 28 March. Fighting took place on the outskirts of the capital, in Cuscatancingo, Apopa, Cuidad Delgado, Soyapango, San Marcos, Mejicanos and San Antonio Abad. Whilst Ambassador Hinton noted that the guerrilla actions were marked by 'intensity and daring', they were nevertheless, unable to sustain more than 10 hours of combat and some of the columns were almost annihilated in ambushes, the survivors falling back into the Cerro de Guazapa.[17] If the March FMLN offensive did not achieve the desired results, it was able to take advantage of the dispersal of the FAES, obliged to protect the conduct of the elections throughout the country and only the lack of coordination between its forces, prevented it from achieved success.

If the elections could not take place normally in more than 22 localities in the east and north, mainly in the Morazan, San Vicente, San Miguel, Usulatan and Chalatenango departments, on election day, a record number of Salvadorans voted – according to some sources, 85 percent of the population. The FMLN failed to significantly disrupt the elections, except in the areas it controlled. It was a success for the Salvadoran government but also for the Reagan administration.

However, the compulsory vote for civilians and the control of the electoral process by the security forces qualified this triumphalism. Above all, the fear that the *Alianza Republicana Nacionalista*

(Nationalist Republican Alliance or ARENA), founded by Roberto D'Aubuisson, would prevail against the PDC, pushed the CIA to spend US$2 million to ensure the success of the latter. Victory for D'Aubuisson, suspected of colluding with death squads, would have meant the end of US Congress support for continued aid to El Salvador and the tipping of part of the population to the FMLN side[18]. Despite its electoral victory, the PDC was in opposition within the Constituent Assembly since ARENA was allied with other small Right-wing parties to obtain the majority. Under pressure from Washington, an agreement was reached between ARENA and the PDC. This Apaneca Pact led to the appointment of Alvaro Magaña as the country's provisional president.

Torola I, April 1982

The organisation of the March 1982 elections determined the military operations at the beginning of the year. The FMLN sought to bring the fighting to the towns in order to disrupt the polls whilst the FAES launched offensives around vital economic zones and towns. They were mainly concentrated on the central fringe of the country, in the Jucuaran region, the Cerros de San Pedro, the Chinchontepec and Guazapa volcanoes where 2,000 to 3,000 men and five 101mm guns intervened from 22 February to 3 March. These operations only succeeded in keeping the guerrillas away from the big cities.

After the fighting in Usulutan, San Vicente, San Miguel, in the Chalatenango and the Cerro de Guazapa, the FAES again turned their attention to the north of Morazan department where Villalobos decided to concentrate the ERP forces to train the embryo of strategic mobile forces. For the FMLN, the failure of the operation against Usulutan marked the defeat of the ERP's insurrectionary strategy. It then decided to carry out a continuous offensive to conquer the countryside and force the FAES to concentrate in the cities. It was a question of applying henceforth, the strategy of protracted people's war with the encirclement of the cities by the countryside, according to the Maoist model. From now on, the FMLN wanted to confront the military in large operations and sought the decisive battle that would lead to the collapse of the FAES.[19]

From April to May 1982, the guerrillas remained on the defensive, limiting themselves to small operations of harassment, ambushes and sabotage. The only major attack took place on 3 April with the destruction of the San Isidro Labrador garrison in the Chalatenango department where 35 soldiers were killed.[20] In Morazan department, whilst Corinto and Jucuaran were in the hands of the FAES, the guerrillas controlled Meanguera. To improve its positions in the event of a new large scale military operation, the ERP decided to seize Cerro Palacios, a position defended by an infantry section 2km east of Jocoaitique.

About 225 fighters, led by Commander Bracamonte, were mobilised for this action. They were in their attack positions on the morning of 6 April when the order arrived not to attack and to withdraw as quickly as possible. Nevertheless, a platoon of 25 guerrillas decided not to obey. It went on the attack and managed to seize the first defences before withdrawing. FAES reinforcements arrived from Jocoaitique and surrounded the forces of Bracamonte who did not take part in the attack. Bracamonte and his men managed to retreat to Arambala whilst the platoon that attacked Cerro Palacio

Wounded ERP guerrilla captured by Atlacatl Battalion in San Miguel department. (Albert Grandolini Collection)

Despite its military qualities which made it an elite unit, the BIRI Atlacatl was put into difficulty by the guerrillas forces as shown by the failure of Operation Torola I. (Albert Grandolini Collection)

was decimated, with only two survivors. This disaster caused violent debates to determine the responsibilities. It took the arrival of Villalobos in El Mozote to avoid a bloodbath between the military leaders of the ERP whilst the FAES were preparing a new operation in this region.[21]

Operation Torola I again targeted northern Morazan to regain control of Meanguera, a small town of a thousand inhabitants 50km north of San Fernando Gotera, then to advance north-east to the La Guacamaya area and north towards Jocoaitique. For this operation, the FAES mobilising an infantry company from the 3rd Infantry Brigade, Commandos from the 6th Infantry Brigade, two companies from BIRI Atlacatl, a squadron of paratroopers and an artillery battery, in effect approximately 800 military.

The first military action of the Belloso Battalion occurred on 24 May 1982 when it was sent to the province of Chalatenango. However, the guerrillas evaded combat and after almost 30 days of operation, they returned to their headquarters. (Albert Grandolini Collection)

The forces departed from Osicala 18km north of San Francisco Gotera for an encirclement manoeuvrer supported by Fouga Magisters, A-37-Bs and helicopters. The FAES destroyed three guerrilla camps and on the evening of 24 April 1982, they occupied Meanguera and Jocoaitique. For its part, the ERP decided not to retreat towards Joateca or Las Mesas. Comandante Bracamonte received the order to occupy the Cerro Los Ortiz and to keep it at all costs with his column reinforced by 200 militiamen from the sector. The column of 200 men of Commander Che Guevara had to disrupt the military forces advancing north from Delicias de Concepcion. Further north, Comandante Irra's column defended the area near the Rio Las Marias south of Arambala. In the Cerro Convenio, a strategic place that protected the sector where Radio Venceremos and the ERP command post were located, there were forces of which the FAES did not know the existence – the columns of Goyo Negro and Cirilo which consisted of 100 men each. Thus with 800 fighters in the area, the guerrillas had the numerical advantage.

On 25 April, the BIRI Atlacatl continued its advance north-east towards Cerro El Tablon whilst the paratroopers progressed towards Cerro El Pajarito east of Meanguera. Whilst the latter end up reaching the Sapo River without difficulty, the BIRI Atlacatl encountered increasingly violent resistance. The next day, it was the paratroopers who had to face the guerrillas who managed to stop them. On the 27th, an infantry company of the 3rd Brigade advanced north towards the Las Marias River but had to face the guerrillas south of Jocoaitique. The entire area between Arambala, Jocoaitique, Meanguera and the banks of the Sapo River, was bombarded by artillery and by the FAS.

On the 28th, the paratroopers headed for the Las Mesas hill, south-east of Poza Honda, whilst on their right, advanced the BIRI Atlacatl which was to conquer the Cerro El Tablon. Commander Che Guevara observed the progress of the paratroopers and organised a night attack against them. The action was violent, the fighting was so close that it prevented the support of artillery and aviation. On the morning of the 29th, the paratroopers' situation was desperate. The guerrilla forces tried to surround them, forcing them to withdraw towards the BIRI Atlacatl. All of the FAES retreated to the banks of the Torola River, protected by a BIRI Atlacatl counter-attack. The same day, a column of 80 men arrived from the south, further strengthening the numerical advantage of the FMLN. The FAES finally received the order to cross the Torola River south of Meanguera, which was carried out on 1st May.

Operation Torola I was a failure for the FAES. The fighting was violent, the paratroopers and the BIRI Atlacatl had 60 wounded, eight dead and one missing. Above all, the FMLN could not be defeated or driven out of the region. The ERP managed to keep control of its *retaguardia* in Morazan and to rout, for the first time, a major FAES offensive.[22] After this success, the leadership of the FMLN planned to launch a major attack and its leaders met in Nicaragua to prepare for the 'Comandante Gonzalo' military campaign.

Operation Dominguez

In June 1982, following the example of Operation Torola I in Morazan, the FAES launched a major offensive in the Chalatenango department, employing some 6,000 men with the support of the Honduran Armed Forces to cover the border and prevent the escape from the guerrillas. On 29 May 1982, the BIRI Belloso, under the command of Lieutenant Colonel Miguel Antonio Méndez, carried out its first military action with a classic operation to search and destroy FAPL positions in the south-east of the Chalatenango department. On the 30th, the BIRI was transported by UH-1H helicopters to the border with Honduras. Meanwhile, the BIRI Atlacatl and a squadron of paratroopers departed from Nombre de Jesus to head north. Units of the 4th Infantry Brigade and BIRI Atonal left San José Las Flores and Nueva Trinitad a few days later to advance north-west. At least one BIRI Atlacatl company landed by helicopters on the Honduran side of the border, in front of La Cañada north of Arcatao, to prevent the enemy from fleeing towards Honduras. The objective of the operation was to surprise and destroy the units of the FMLN which would be blocked between the forces of the FAES coming from three different directions.

The guerrillas nevertheless, avoided combat and managed to withdraw westward to Nueva Trinidad to escape the pincers formed by the paratroopers and the BIRI Atlacatl. Fighting mostly boiled down to skirmishes. The soldiers destroyed 12 guerrilla camps, including that of Cerro Chicilco, from where Carpio fled to Honduras. The operation ended on 9 June with Carpio's decision to break through to escape the encirclement. If the FAPL choose not to resist the military, it was because its leaders were preparing a major offensive in the areas of Las Vueltas and El Jicaro and wanted to preserve their forces.[23] Operation Dominguez cost the lives of 15 soldiers and was accompanied by the military's massacre of hundreds of civilians in what is called Guinda de Mayo.[24]

Undersecretary of Defence Colonel Castillo was captured by guerrillas after his plane was shot down as he wanted to reach San Fernando on 17 June 1982. (Author's Collection)

Contrary to the Chalatenango and Morazan departments, in that of Cabaña, the FMLN did not manage to increase its manpower, nor receive the support of the population. This situation allowed the DM 2, under the command of Lieutenant Colonel Sigfrido Ochoa Pérez, to maintain constant pressure on the guerrillas, especially since it sometimes received support from paratroopers or BIRI during search and destruction operations. Thus, from 10 June 1982, a squadron of paratroopers and a squadron of cavalry led a seven-day operation in this department. In the San Felipe sector, the paratroopers discovered a guerrilla column. To destroy it, they used mortars and called on the FAS, which sent a Fouga fighter-bomber to bomb it but it nevertheless, managed to flee. Paratroopers also discovered an empty FMLN camp before returning to Ilopango Air Base.[25]

The 'Comandante Gonzalo' Campaign, June 1982

The second half of 1982 was difficult for the FAES. Despite US military aid, the FMLN inflicted a series of defeats on them which left them in a difficult situation. However, they continued to launch large scale operations in areas held by the FMLN. These generally yielded few results except for numerous massacres of civilians, such as in El Calabozo, in the San Vicente department on 22 August 1982, where the BIRI Atlacatl killed over 200 people.

On 5 June 1982, the ERP launched the 'Comandante Gonzalo' campaign, the objective of which was to reduce the pressure on the Chalatenango by attracting a large FAES unit to defeat it in an ambush to the north, near the Torola River.[26] On the night of 5 June, the guerrillas began to attack Perquin and its garrison of 70 soldiers. On the morning of the 6th, the garrison managed to flee but at the same time the 6th Infantry Brigade sent Commandos as reinforcements which arrived in San Fernando to then move on Perquin. On the way, they faced the rebel forces led by Jehova Marques alias Cirilo. When the soldiers learned the garrison had been able to flee, they decided to return to San Fernando to take refuge there and wait for reinforcements.[27] The ERP decided to lay siege to the city when it knew that FAES reinforcements had arrived in Torola, 10km south of San Fernando. Two infantry companies of the 3rd Infantry Brigade and a support company of the DM-4, approximately 300 to 350 soldiers, had to rescue the besieged Commandos.

On 9 June, these reinforcements were stopped by the guerrillas in Cerro Moscardan, also called Moscarron. As night fell, the FAES command decided to wait until morning to continue the advance. meanwhile, a group of a hundred FMLN fighters was formed to march towards El Moscarron under the command of Claudio Armijo. On the morning of the 10th, helicopters that had come to support the soldiers were forced to flee before the intensity of guerrilla fire.[28] Until the 11th, the soldiers first tried to advance to join the besieged Commandos in San Fernando then they fought for their survival while the guerrillas had succeeded in isolating and surrounding them. Finally, on the 11th, the company of the 3rd Infantry Brigade and the support company of DM-4 were destroyed. The FAES had 76 dead and 42 soldiers were taken prisoner. They suffered an unprecedented disaster.[29]

On 15 June, the FAES General Staff was forced to transfer 3,500 men to Morazan to rescue the Commandos and regain control of northern Morazan. At the same time, the FAS received, from the United States, six A-37 Dragonfly fighter-bombers and four O-2A reconnaissance aircraft.[30] On the 17th, the Undersecretary of Defence, Colonel Francisco Adolfo Castillo, decided to go to San Fernando to boost the morale of the Commandos defending the

A-37Bs parked at Ilopango Air Base. A mixture of A-37B and OA-37B were supplied from June 1982 and these US light attack aircraft were used for the first time in the Morazan department. (Albert Grandolini Collection)

city. In the afternoon, the Hughes-500D helicopter in which he was travelling was shot down a few miles north-west of San Fernando. Colonel Castillo was captured the next day by the guerrillas as he tried to flee the area to reach Honduras.

On the 18th, the new A-37s made their baptism of fire by bombarding the guerrilla positions around San Fernando. In the city, the Commandos, led by Colonel Carranza de Leon, who had run out of ammunition, decided to withdraw to Honduras from where they could join El Salvador. The guerrillas then controlled Perquin, Arambala, Torola, Oscicala and San Fernando. It was not until the 24th that the FAES regained control of San Fernando and Perquin after difficult fights led by the BIRI Atlacatl, Atonal and Belloso.[31] For its part, the FMLN claimed that its campaign enabled it to recover 160 weapons, take prisoner 44 soldiers whilst 600 were killed or wounded.[32] The FAES revealed at this time, their powerlessness to thwart the attacks of the guerrillas. They had to withdraw without fulfilling their mission of rescuing the Undersecretary of Defense, thus accentuating the humiliation suffered.

The situation was not much better in Chalatenango where on 2 July, the FAPL forces launched a campaign to drive out the garrisons from this department and support the ERP troops who were under strong pressure in Morazan. The first garrison attacked was Ojos de Agua, 18km north of Chalatenango. The rifle company of the DM-1 which protected this locality, did not receive reinforcements and its captain decided to abandon it in small groups. Some managed to reach Chalatenango, others Honduras. FAPL forces also occupied, without encountering resistance, El Carrizal, Las Vueltas and Arcatao.[33]

The war then boiled down to a game of cat-and-mouse between the guerrillas and the FAES. When the latter concentrated its efforts on Morazan, the guerrillas responded by occupying the now unguarded areas of Chalatenango and vice versa. This situation was not to the liking of US military advisors who advocated a change of tactics. They proposed to erode and isolate the guerrilla forces by preventing them from receiving weapons, driving them out of important economic areas and pushing them back to their *retaguardias* where they could be destroyed by political and military means.

The FAES implemented the suggestions of the American advisors between June and November 1982. In order to prevent the supply of the FMLN, Navy patrols multiplied on the coasts whilst on land, intense night patrol activity was set up, particularly in the Cabañas and Usulutan departments. Finally, major search operations were taking place in the San Vicente, Cuscutlan, San Miguel and Usulutan departments. These actions caused a decrease in the FMLN military operations between July and September, compensated by an increase in sabotage actions.

Nevertheless, on 7 August, the FMLN launched Operation Comandante Manlio Armijo in the San Miguel department. A guerrilla column, commanded by Javier, attacks GN outposts in Ciudad Barrios, a city of about 20,000 people. At 3:00 p.m. the last GN surrendered their weapons. Meanwhile, Licho and his men were a few kilometres away, waiting for FAES reinforcements from San Miguel. The forces of the 3rd Infantry Brigade fell into the ambush. Explosive charges put the trucks out of service and after three hours of fighting, the last soldiers fled. A few days later, the FMLN seized the town of Yamabal in Morazan then on 22 August, the San Carlos Hacienda on the Cacahuatique volcano, capturing 18 rifles and a 57mm cannon. These various actions of the guerrillas during the month of August represented the loss of more than one FAES company between prisoners, dead and wounded.[34]

After the capture of Yamabal, the FAES began a vast operation in the San Vicente department with 3,000 soldiers. They took back Yambala, destroyed two guerrilla camps and a hospital and seized arms caches. On 19 August, with Operation Teniente Coronel Mario Azenon Palma, 1,600 soldiers including the BIRI Atlacatl launched an assault on the Cerros de San Pedro in the San Vicente department. The guerrilla forces managed to flee and it was under these conditions that BIRI Atlacatl massacred more than 200 civilians in El Calabozo.[35] Despite these reactions from the FAES, the FMLN resumed the offensive in October with renewed vigour.

7
THE RISE OF THE FMLN, SEPTEMBER 1982 – MAY 1983

The end of 1982 marked a qualitative leap in the military organisation of the FMLN. The guerrillas were getting stronger and now had the means to form battalion-sized units, sometimes even a brigade. It now had the ability to launch major strategic offensives and put the FAES in difficulty.

Towards the Revolutionary Army

The FMLN forces were undergoing transformations linked to their growth and the adoption of new tactics. According to the CIA, the strength of the FMLN on 1982 was 4,000 to 5,000 combatants and 5,000 to 10,000 militiamen.[1] At its peak in 1983–1984, the FMLN would have around 14,000 regular combatants and around 6,000 militiamen.[2] This increase in manpower made it possible to train support, artillery and sapper units, as well as a medical service with hospitals. A school of communication was created which used small radios and many women became radio operators for the platoons and columns.

The tactical organisation of the guerrillas, which were initially based on platoons acting independently of each other, changed to give rise to columns formed of two sections each. These were composed of two platoons of between 80 and 120 men, who then gathered into battalions and mobile groups down to the level of a brigade. These Mobile Strategic Forces formed the backbone of the FMLN military apparatus.[3]

It was during the spring of 1982 that the FMLN was able to build brigade-sized military units (1,500 men) with the formation of the Rafael Arce Zablah Brigade (BRAZ) from the ERP and *Agrupacion de Batallones Felipe Peña Mendoza* (Felipe Peña Mendoza Battalion Group or ABFPM) of the FPL. The BRAZ kept most of its units in the east of the country and a smaller force in the west. The ABFPM with four battalions of 250 men each, operated in the Chalatenango,

The FMLN Mobile Forces			
Organisation	**Units**	**Subdivision**	**Locations**
ERP	Rafael Arce Zablah Brigade		
	Augustin Ticas Battalion (BAT)		
	Bruno Caballero Battalion (BBC)		
	Heroic Workers Battalion (BTH)		
	Amilcar Hernandez Battalion (BAH)		
	Juan Carlos Battalion (BJC)		
	Heroes of Cutumay Camones Battalion (BHCC)		
FPL	Felipe Peha Medoza Battalion Group	- Juan Méndez Battalion (BJM) or X-21 - Alejandro Solano Battalion (BAS) or K-93 - Andrés Torres Sanchez Battalion (BATS) or SS-20 - Ernesto Morales Sandoval Battalion (BEMS) or S-7	Chalatenango Cerros San Pedro (San Vicente Department)
FAL	Rafael Aguihada Carranza Battalion (BRAC)		Cerro Guazapa
	Rafael A. Torres Battalion (BRAT)		Chalatenango Cerros San Pedro (San Vicente Department)
RN	Carlos Arias Battalion (BCA)		Cerro Guazapa
	Sergio Hernandez Battalion (BSH)		
	Dolores Ardin Battalion (BDA		
PRTC	Luis Alberto Diaz Detachment (DLAD)		Morazan Cerros San Pedro (San Vicente Department)

During 1982, the growth in guerrilla numbers allowed the FMLN to form units the size of a battalion or a brigade, such as the Rafael Arce Zablah Brigade or BRAZ whose fighter traces a slogan on a wall to announce his glory. (Albert Grandolini Collection)

Cabañas, San Vicente and Zacatecoluca departments. The FAL organised the Rafael Aguiñada Carranza Battalion (BRAC) with 250 men, which operated in the centre of the country and in the areas of Guazapa and Cinquera. The FAR-LP formed the *Detachment Luis Adalberto Diaz* (DLAD) with 250 men which operated in the area of the Chichontepec volcano and Cerros San Pedro in the San Vicente, although it also had forces in the Usulutan. Finally, the FARN set up the Carlos Arias Battalion with 250 men in the areas of Guazapa and Cinquera and tried to form a second battalion, but which only had a column of 100 to 120 men in the east of the country.[4]

In two years, the structure of the guerrillas had become more complex. It also had local units, stationed mainly in the Cerro de Guazapa, the Morazan and Chalatenango departments, which defended the *retaguardias* and formed the bulk of the troops during major attacks against the FAES. These units were linked to a specific territory that they knew well. Militias were also local groups but whose members were not full-time combatants. They were responsible for sabotage, defence missions, military harassment and intelligence.[5]

Guerrilla FMLN in San Vicente department. The latter became the stake of a fierce struggle between the FMLN and the FAES for its control. (Albert Grandolini Collection)

The FMLN was also equipped with special forces, the FES, permanent elite units, created on the Vietnamese model, which had to operate both in rural and urban areas. One of their first actions was carried out by combat swimmers who blew up the Puente de Oro in October 1981.[6]

From mid-1982, with its two brigades and three battalions armed with significant firepower thanks to 57 and 90mm Recoilless Rifles, 60, 81 and 120mm mortars and M-2 and M-60 machine guns, the FMLN could challenge the FAES for control of the territory.[7]

The *Heroes y Martires de Octubre* Campaign, Autumn 1982

From mid-1982 to early 1984, the FMLN launched and developed major offensives, while the FAES found themselves in a defensive position. In October 1982, the FMLN began the campaign *Heroes y martires de octubre* whose goal was to isolate the territory east of the Lempa River, first by destroying all the bridges over this river but above all, by taking control of Usulutan and San Vicente departments which were precisely crossed by the Lempa River. For this, the guerrillas had to involve the FAES in major operations against their retaguardias in the north whilst small attacks had to weaken the vital economic agricultural centres of San Vicente and

At the end of 1982, the structure and equipment of the FMLN forces gave them more and more the appearance of a conventional army. (Albert Grandolini Collection)

Usulutan. By ruining the economy, the government would be crippled and the eastern third of the country would be isolated under the control of the FMLN.

The campaign began on 9 October in northern Chalatenango when, after two days of fighting, the FAPL occupied Las Vueltas and El Jicaro, routing a DM-1 company reinforced by GN agents, about 120 men including 19 were killed and 58 taken prisoner. The FAES decided to respond by sending the Cazadores battalions Cazadores Sierpe of the DM-1, Cayaguanca of the 4th Brigade and Pipil of the 2nd Brigade to the area. But these forces were pushed back by the guerrillas.

At the same time, the ERP attacked in the north of Morazan and occupied San Fernando, Torola and Perquin. In Perquin, a 6th Brigade company which held the city, resisted then tried to flee towards Llano El Muerto where it fell into an ambush. Its commander and 44 soldiers were captured. The ERP forces were only stopped by another infantry company near Jocoaitique. During this offensive, the FMLN took full control of northern Morazan for 81 days.

The FAES launched a series of operations to take back these different localities. In Chalatenango, the Cazdores Battalion Sierpe and other units had to recapture Las Vueltas and El Jicaro. These large forces of around 3,500 soldiers, however, were unable to defeat the FAPL troops. In Morazan, FAES units, gathering 4,000 men, were responsible for repelling the advance of the guerrillas on San Francisco Gotera. On 25 October, the FAPL attacked the town without inflicting much damage on the defenders. A month later, it was attacked again by the guerrillas, this time using 81mm mortars. The FAPL were also seeking to interrupt traffic on the Litoral Highway in order to further isolate the east of the country. The BIRI Atonal was responsible for keeping the highway open, thus achieving one of the objectives of the guerrillas, namely the dispersal of FAES forces which, for political and strategic reasons, could not accept the closure of an important road.[8]

On 2 November, joint FARN and ERP forces organised an ambush against the CICFA support company. This unit of 125 soldiers, reinforced by forces from a Commando company, advanced towards Corinto from Sociedad and was ambushed south of the city. After two days of fighting, the soldiers were defeated. They had 35 killed and 62 captured including two officers.[9]

On 10 November, the FAES sent a new force of 5,000 men into Chalatenango to reseize the small towns of Las Vueltas, El Jicaro, San José La Flores, Arcatao, La Laguna and Nueva Trinitad. The Cazadores Battalions Cayaguanca, Sierpe, Jaguar, units of the 3rd Infantry Brigade and a GN company, fought fierce battles that caused them many losses to recover the lost cities. On 19 November, the mission was finally accomplished. meanwhile, 4,000 soldiers including the BIRI Atlacatl, Atonal and Belloso left for Morazan to seize Torola, Perquin and San Fernando while the guerrillas besieged Jocoaitique.[10] The fighting lasted until January 1983 and the guerrillas often put the soldiers in serious difficulty.

The FMLN decided to get as close as possible to the big cities in the departments where it was powerful. In the north of the San Miguel department, the ERP approached San Luis de la Reyna, Ciudad Barrios, Carolina and San Gerardo, whilst in that of La Union, it was close to Anamoros, Poloros and Nueva Esparta. On 26 October, the guerrillas attacked Carolina in the north of the San Miguel department and Joateca in Morazan. On 7 November, RN forces informed the ERP that they had contained a FAES company on the Gotera-Corinto Road. Licho and his men left immediately, improvising a plan to besiege and destroy this unit. The heaviest combat took place when the guerrillas stormed the heights defended by heavy artillery and machine guns. The FAS intervened and bombed the canton of San Felipe. After a long day of fighting, the guerrillas prevailed, taking 62 prisoners and capturing two 120mm mortars and two .50 calibre machine guns.[11]

FAES soldiers in Chalatenango on 1982. (Albert Grandolini Collection)

The small locality of Anamoros, in the La Union department, appeared to be strategic since it was a communication node and as such, an important battle staked for the FMLN, which sought to control the entire region in order to expand its area of operation and drive out FAES concentrations from northern Morazan. At the beginning of November 1982, Anamoros was defended by 40 members of the GN and the Civil Defence. On 26 November, the guerrillas attacked Nueva Esparta, Anamoros, Poloros and Lislique, which they managed to conquer after taking 53 prisoners. The FAES sent the BIRI Atonal and the 6th Infantry Brigade to restore the situation, but they fell into ambushes and were repulsed. On 28 November, a paratrooper squadron landed south of Anamoros whilst a company of the 6th Brigade advanced from El Sauce and the BIRI Atonal, from Santa Rosa de Lima. The paratroopers progressed to Anamoros, then Nueva Esparta and finally Lislique, carrying out sweeps throughout the region. The operations lasted eight days without the paratroopers having any losses whilst the BIRI Atonal and Cuscatlan, which regained control of Anamoros, Nueva Esparta and Lislique, had 15 dead and 40 wounded.

On 23 December, the FAES seized Carolina north of the San Miguel department. The next day, the BIRI Atlacatl headed south to join Ciudad Barrios whilst the paratroopers remained in Carolina. When they learned the presence of ERP forces in San Luis de la Reyna, they decided to attack them on 24 December. They asked help from the FAS and an Ouragan fighter bombed the guerrilla positions before the paratrooper's attack. The guerrillas flew towards San Gerardo whilst the FAES entered San Luis de la Reyna.[12]

From 14 October, the FMLN also launched a campaign of sabotage throughout the country. The eastern part of El Salvador was practically paralysed, without transport or electricity. There was a great shortage of fuel because more than a dozen tanker trucks that provided supplies were destroyed, water was rationed, and the railway was paralysed by the destruction of bridges and locomotives. In the central area were the four departments most affected by

A truck burnt by ERP on the Pan-American Highway. (Albert Grandolini Collection)

FLMN Fighters in Usulutan on 1983. (Albert Grandolini Collection)

blackouts: San Vicente, Cabañas, Cuscatlan and Chalatenango. In March 1983, the FMLN succeeded in depriving 60 percent of the population of electricity.[13] In the capital, sabotage caused the reduction of the urban transport service, the energy of the capital was at less than 50 percent of its normal level and sometimes, it was completely interrupted. Thousands of telephone lines were out of service. In the western part of the country, there was a partial paralysis of transport with the destruction of vans, buses and trucks loaded with coffee whilst electricity was rationed and commercial transport from Guatemala was interrupted.[14]

The autumn 1982 campaign once again demonstrated the FMLN's ability to coordinate its forces simultaneously on all fronts, to annihilate several FAES units and to operate in new theatres of operations. Whilst units were tasked with destroying government forces in Chalatenango and Morazan departments, others carried out harassing actions in the Usulutan and San Vicente departments and in the Guazapa area. Meanwhile, commando operations were carried out in the areas controlled by the FAES with the attacks on the PH garrison in San Salvador or the oil refinery in the port of Acajutla. The FMLN had the military ascendancy and expanded the territory under its control. In November, it controlled 28 of the 33 municipalities of Chalatenango department.[15]

Faced with the actions of the FMLN, the FAES operations were reactive, fewer in number and shorter in time. The military were unable to attack simultaneously in Chalatenango and Morazan department and until the end of the year, they were unable to penetrate northern Morazan. The FAES reacted very slowly to attacks and did not adopt the counter-insurgency tactics that the situation demanded. A US military advisor remarked:

> The senior officers still have not accepted the fact that conventional tactics cannot be used to defeat the insurgency. They still insist on conducting multi-battalion operations which have proved ineffective. They do not have sufficient troops, mobility or logistical capability to seal the insurgents in an area and eliminate them. When they try such operations, the guerrillas simply exfiltrate through the lines at will and strike elsewhere.[16]

According to General Wallace H. Nutting, then Commander-in-Chief of the US Southern Command, the situation in El Salvador in late 1982 and early 1983 was dire. After completing his term, he said that during those few months, 'everything was on the verge of falling apart. The Leftist guerrillas ... were very strong. The armed forces did not yet have their act together'.[17] The FAES were going through a deep crisis, their losses had increased considerably. They were 3,840 men in 1982, in effect 1,040 dead and more than 2,800 injured, compared to 1,600 in 1981 – an increase of 58.4 percent.[18] Faced with this situation, on 10 October 1982, the Minister of Defence, General José Guillermo Garcia announced that the FAES would no longer seek to seize the localities occupied by the guerrillas which were not of military importance. Instead, they should focus their attention on controlling larger cities, leaving the strategic initiative to the FMLN.

The *Heroes Revolucionarios de Enero* Campaign, January – May 1983

If the FAES adopted a defensive posture in 1982, it was to have the time necessary to accumulate forces and organise them on the US counter-insurgency model. This reorganisation did not fail to create tensions as military setbacks accumulated. On 27 October, the provisional president, Alvaro Magaña, met with the high command to study the negotiation proposals made by the FMLN. This meeting, which lasted nearly eight hours, took place at the time of the visit to El Salvador of the US Undersecretary of Defense, Fred Ikle. On 10 November, the FAES command was changed and on 17 December, many commanders were relieved of their duties and replaced.[19] For his part, General Waghelstein, commander of the Milgroup, demanded the replacement of the least capable regional commanders, which provoked angry reactions within the FAES.

On 7 January 1983, Lieutenant Colonel Sigifredo Ochoa Pérez, commander of DM-2 in La Cabañas, mutinied and demanded the resignation of the Minister of Defence, General Guillermo Garcia, as well as the end of American interference in El Salvador. Ochoa, one

Lieutenant Colonel Sigifredo Ochoa Pérez, commander of DM-2 in La Cabañas, one of the best Salvadoran officers, opposed the interference of American military advisors in the FAES organisation. (Albert Grandolini Collection)

General Carlos Eugenio Vides Casanova became Minister of Defence at the beginning of 1983. Under his leadership, the FAES accelerated their transformation and adopted a US counter-insurgency strategy. (Albert Grandolini Collection)

During 1983, the FMLN extended its control in the Morazan and Chalatenango departments, in particular by seizing numerous localities. (Albert Grandolini Collection)

of the most efficient officers of the FAES, was close to D'Aubuisson, the leader of the extreme Right. He received the support of the FAS whilst the commanders of the 3 BIRI declared themselves neutral. The FAS Chief of Staff, Colonel Bustillo, and the commander of the 1st Brigade, Colonel Blandón, refused to recognise Garcia's authority, holding him responsible for the continued failures against the guerrillas. Finally, the Minister of Defence resigned on 13 March to be replaced by General Eugenio Vides Casanova. The latter carried out a profound restructuring of his ministry so that it could effectively direct the conduct of the war. He appointed Adolfo Onecifro Blandón as head of the General Staff and replaced the least capable local commanders.[20]

Whilst the FAES faced this internal crisis, the '*Heroes revolucionarios de enero*' (January revolutionaries Heroes) offensive began on 10 January 1983 in the Morazan department where the guerrillas jostled the 300 soldiers defending Jocoaitique, who had to withdraw a few kilometres to the south. The pressure from the ERP nevertheless grew stronger and, on the 15th, after three days of fighting, the FAES were about to be surrounded and had to fall back towards Meanguera which was seized by the guerrillas on the 16th.[21] On the 12th, it had already seized Cacaopera where the garrison was attacked with RPG-2s.[22] Soon, the FMLN controlled seven localities in northern Morazan: Torola, San Fernando, Perquin, Arambala, Meanguera, Jocoatique, Villa del Rosario, Joateca, Cacaopera, Corinto, Guatajiagua, Sensembra and Yamabal. In the northern region of San Miguel department, they controlled Carolina and in La Union, Anamoros, Poloros, Lislique, and Nueva Esparta.

With Operation Escalante Acevedo, the FAES sent 3,000 men to get back the lost ground north of the Torola River. Most belong to the 3rd Infantry Brigade but there were also the BIRI Atlacatl, Atonal, Belloso and the Cazadores battalions, Cuscatlan and Pipil. The losses of the soldiers were important but on 21 January, the BIRI Atonal, commanded by Colonel Herson Calito, succeeded in seizing Meanguera. During the night, the FES managed to blow up the BIRI command post whilst a violent counter-attack pushed back the soldiers who were forced to recross the Torola River. New reinforcements arrived bringing the FAES to 6,000 men. Nevertheless, for a week the guerrillas managed to resist the assaults of the soldiers who had failed to cross the Torola River. Eventually they began to withdraw.[23]

The FAES decided to apply a new strategy to the north of Morazan, which consisted of carrying out constant patrols with the best troops from a temporary base set up in Perquin. The BIRI Belloso, reinforced by units of the 3rd Infantry Brigade, was responsible for this mission. On 17 February, the ERP ambushed a patrol just 12km from Perquin. Three soldiers were killed and five injured. Colonel Méndez, who commanded the BIRI Belloso, asked for the evacuation of Perquin because he feared the FMLN sought to make the capture of this city a new Dien Bien Phu battle.[24] On the 23rd, under intense pressure from the guerrillas, the BIRI Belloso abandoned the locality which passed under the control of the ERP as well as the north of Morazan. On the Torola River south bank, it was reinforced by the Cazadores battalion Morazan in order to prevent the guerrillas from advancing on the capital of the department. During the fighting in February, the BIRI Belloso lost a company, annihilated by the guerrillas, during combat in the canton of San Simon.[25]

Yugoslavian-built M-56 105mm ready to shell occupied Berlin Town on February 1983. (Albert Grandolini Collection)

The FMLN maintained its control over other areas and towns in the Usulutan department. It even increased it on 6 February, by seizing Jiquilisco, a city near the ocean, cutting rail and highway links. The Jiquilisco garrison was limited to 30 GN, the rest of the troops having been sent to reconquer Berlin. On 14 February, the FALP ambushed a patrol of 45 CIIFA soldiers a few kilometres north of Zacatecoluca. The FAES lost 41 men, killed or captured during this operation. The FMLN again demonstrated its superiority and its ability to manoeuvrer and attack.[28]

At the beginning of March, the FAES high command installed the Jaguar battalion as the first line of defence between the FMLN forces and the capital of the Morazan department. The guerrillas went on the attack against their forces on 2 March, carrying out numerous assaults against the garrisons of Osicala and Delicias de Concepcion in addition to other FAES positions south of the Torola River. They managed to surround 600 soldiers whilst the troops defending the garrisons, dispersed and ambushes welcomed the reinforcements. The high command had to send into Morazan department, the BIRI Atonal, Paratroopers and Cazadores troops.[26]

Taking advantage of the FAES concentration in Morazan, the FMLN went on the offensive in other regions. In the La Cabaña department, ERP troops attacked and seized San Isidro on 30 March. To recapture the locality, the FAES sent part of the BIRI Belloso but on 1st April, the 250 men of the Comandante Gonzalo Battalion of the Rafael Arce Zablah Brigade managed to almost annihilate the military completely – 43 soldiers died whilst the guerrillas only had three killed and 14 wounded. Finally, the BIRI Belloso was replaced by the BIRI Atlacatl.[27] Elsewhere in Chalatenango department, on 8 January the FMLN seized Tejutla. It even launched actions in the capital, the most spectacular of which was the attack on the 1st Brigade headquarters and other military and police targets on the outskirts of San Salvador on 28 January. The attack, organised from the Guazapa volcano, lasted all night and was the first that the capital has suffered since the 1982 elections.

In the Usulutan department, the guerrillas seized San Augustin on 28 January. On 30 January, ERP forces captured Berlin, a city of 30,000 inhabitants, only defended by the GN. The news of this success by the FMLN fell like a bomb, demonstrating that the guerrillas had enough strength to simultaneously stop the FAES in Morazan department, launch operations in various regions and occupy an important city. The FAS was the first to counter-attack, bombarding the city. The guerrillas pushed back the reinforcements sent by the FAES and only withdrew on 3 February, when the arrival of the BIRI Belloso was announced. Only rearguard fighting took place in which a US military advisor was wounded, which caused a scandal in the United States since the Reagan administration insisted relentlessly that advisors be expressly denied access to combat areas.

The Cuscatlan Battle

These actions took place whilst the Battle of Cuscatlan was being fought by the FMLN from the Cerro de Guazapa. In this region, in February 1983, the five formations of the FMLN, which had a unified command there, decided to regroup their forces to allow the creation of military units of the size of a brigade or a battalion. They brought together more than a thousand fighters who set off to attack Suchitoto, a town 44km north-east of the capital and near two hydroelectric dams which provided half of El Salvador's electricity. FAPL and FARN troops attacked the city's 150 defenders whilst other units harassed patrols coming from San Martin, San Salvador and Aguilares. Suchitoto soon found itself surrounded.

The city was attacked on 16 February by 500 guerrillas who succeeded at the same time, in seizing Cerro Tecomatepeque and the city of Oratorio de Concepcion. The FAES were forced to abandon their forward positions to occupy a defensive line on the shores of Lake Suchitlan in order to defend the landing zone where 250 men from the DM-5 and the 1st Airborne squadron disembarked from UH-1H helicopters. This increased the manpower defending Suchitoto to 400 men. These reinforcements attacked the guerrillas who already occupied the south of the city.

On the 20th, the soldiers decided to break the encirclement of Suchitoto and to attack Cerro de Guazapa. The operation, named Guazapa 10, included members of the Santa Ana PN, the GN, the PH, the 1st Infantry Battalion, a DM-1 company, a group of the BIRI Atlacatl, the Cazadores battalion Pipil from the 2nd Infantry Brigade, an armoured squadron and a Cazadores battalion from the DM-2. This force of 4,000 men was commanded by the head of the 1st Infantry Brigade, Colonel Adolfo Onecifero Blandón.

During the first phase of the operation, which lasted three days, the fighting was fierce and the guerrillas put up strong resistance. The second consisted in establishing a double encirclement of the Palo Grande sector and on 24 February, the FARN camp in this area was captured by the Pipil and Atlacatl battalions. Other camps were also seized by the military. The third phase of the operation, that of clearing the area, was entrusted to the BIRI Atlacatl who had to destroy the last guerrillas' redoubts.

After having besieged Suchitoto for three weeks, the loss of the Palo Grande camp forced the guerrillas to withdraw. Accompanied by many civilians but also captured soldiers, the rebels gathered at

Colonel Sigifredo Ochoa (left) and Domingo Monterrosa (right). Monterrosa, who commanded the BIRI Atlacatl, was known to be obsessed with destroying the pro-rebel Radio Venceremos. (Albert Grandolini Collection)

El Roble to cross the road that led from San Martin to Suchitoto. During the night, the enormous column of guerrillas crossed the road to reach the region of Radiola. Colonel Domingo Monterrosa, commander of the BIRI Atlacatl, set off in pursuit as they tried to cross Lake Suchitlan by boat towards Chalatenango department. On the morning of 28 February, the soldiers set an ambush and destroyed a first group of a hundred rebels at El Plan de Tenango south of Suchitoto. To prevent letting the others flee, from 11:00 a.m. until dusk, A-37s bombarded the fleeing guerrillas in all directions, killing around 250. Whilst many soldiers who were prisoners of the guerrillas managed to escape, some were nonetheless executed. During the fighting, thousands of civilians had to find refuge in Honduras in the camps of Mesa Grande and Colomoncagua. According to General Orlando Zepeda, the FAES had about 200 wounded and killed during the operation and the guerrillas had about 400 killed, wounded or missing.[29]

Despite Operation Guazapa 10, the FARN still had their best troops in the Cerro de Guazapa but also their central command headed by Eduardo Sancho alias Fermán Cienfuegos. It was also in their sector that the PRTC main base was located. To maintain the pressure on the Cerro de Guazapa, the FAES sent units of the GN, the Cavalry Regiment, the Airborne Battalion and troops of the 1st Infantry Brigade to carry out Operation Salitre 3. It lasted from 21 April to 14 May with FAES using constant and aggressive patrols. The objective was to expel the FMLN from the area or to force it to concentrate in a sector where it would be subjected to the firepower of the FAES.

In reaction, the FARN, reinforced by a group of FAR-LP, decided to attack the military supply routes. On 5 May, they ambushed the 2nd Airborne Squadron. The fights lasted more than three hours. The paratroopers received support from an A-37B fighter-bomber, but it could not intervene because the positions of each side were too close. Finally, it was the 3rd Airborne Squadron which was sent to rescue its comrades. Among the latter, some managed to flee, but when the 3rd Squadron arrived in Izcanal, it found only corpses and had to face the firepower of the guerrillas which forced it to retreat. It was not until 14 May that the land was finally occupied by the FAES – 10 paratroopers were killed and 31 injured.[30]

At the same time, the FAES launched Operation Relampago in Chalatenango department and recaptured towns such as Concepcion Quezaltepeque and Dulce Nombre. These few successes did not prevent the FMLN, at the start of April, from remaining solidly established in Morazan and Chalatenango departments, or from beginning to occupy solid positions in San Vicente and Usulutan departments. In the latter, it even permanently controlled San Agustín from where it launched frequent incursions against the Litoral Highway. Above all, it was preparing new offensives.

8

THE FAES ON THE VERGE OF DEFEAT, JUNE – DECEMBER 1983

Throughout 1982, the FAES began to develop a counter-insurgency strategy centred on the formation of specialised units, such as the BIRIs, which had the ability to penetrate areas controlled by the FMLN. They were also developing civic action plans, which included the construction of schools, the paving of roads and the provision of health services in areas of strategic and economic value, such as the San Vicente and Usulutan departments where the FMLN sought to establish itself. This policy was put in place when the guerrillas had the initiative but when their strategy of concentration of forces, showed serious limits.

The FMLN Crisis

Although Cuban support for the FMLN did not disappear at any time during the war, it diminished from 1982 to 1983 in the face of threats from Washington, reluctance from Moscow and the impossibility of obtaining a quick victory. All of this led Cuba to recommend that the FMLN leaders promoted a strategy combining armed struggle and negotiation with the government. It tried to persuade the FMLN that it was time to seek an agreement with the government in order to appease the Reagan administration and contribute to guaranteeing the survival of the Nicaraguan revolution. The hardening of US positions also forced the Nicaraguans to moderate their support for the FMLN from 1983 onwards.[1]

The murder of Commander Ana Maria, one of the main FPL leaders, led to the suicide of Cayetano Carpio a week later, causing an internal crisis within the FMLN. (Author's Collection)

US Navy Lieutenant Commander Albert Shaufelberger was the senior US Naval representative at the US Military Group since August 1982. He was shot four times in the head in San Salvador by a FAR-LP urban commando on 25 May 1983. (Albert Grandolini Collection)

The FMLN still had differences within it, particularly concerning the strategy and the objectives of the revolution. For a minority, represented by FPL leader Carpio, the revolution had to be led by a worker-peasant alliance and victory achieved through armed struggle and the use of a protracted people's war strategy. This meant that the FMLN had to refuse to form alliances with other social forces and viewed negotiations with the government with great reservations.

Faced with Carpio, the majority position within the FMLN, defended among others by the PCS secretary general, Schafik Handal, was based on the development of close relations with the most moderate sectors of Christian democracy and on the commitment of a negotiation process to end the war. Carpio's view was rejected by most FMLN commanders who preferred to promote a dual strategy of armed struggle and negotiations, a view supported by Castro. The possibility of seizing power through armed struggle was not excluded, but a second path was open which could end the conflict in a scenario of shared power.[2]

In disagreement with this double strategy, Carpio refused to attend the CG meetings where he was replaced by Mélida Anaya Montes alias Ana Maria, closer to the majority position. Carpio was further isolated when he was outvoted by the commanders of his own organisation at an FPL meeting in Managua in late 1982 or early 1983. The crisis was resolved with the murder of Anaya Montes in Managua on 6 April 1983. An FPL statement initially attributed the crime to the CIA but the murderer turned out to be another guerrilla leader, Roberto Bassaglia, known as Comandante Marcelo, a supporter of Carpio. The leadership of the FMLN tried to hide the real reasons for the murder but a few days later, on 12 April, Carpio committed suicide, apparently because he could not bear the fact that his subordinate had murdered Ana Maria.[3] His death nevertheless, allowed the political opening of the FPL, now in the hands of a younger and more pragmatic generation of militants and a greater cohesiveness within the FMLN.

Despite its internal crisis, the FMLN continued to show great military aggression and on 9 April, it launched the '*Comandante Ana María, juramos vencer*' campaign. The guerrillas seized Santa Rosa de Lima in the La Union department on 29 April. Although they left the city the next day, they managed, before the arrival of the FAES, to blow up six bridges and some high voltage lines. Simultaneously, and very close to the area, the FMLN attacked the El Amatillo international bridge. The fighting was violent and Honduran troops intervened, including a Sherman tank. Finally, the guerrillas managed to blow up the bridge.[4]

On 25 May 1983, the FMLN launched the campaign '*Frente a la agresion de Reagan, El Salvador vencera*'. It began with minor actions such as the attack on the Quebrada Seca bridge on the Pan-American Highway and attacks against FAES positions, such as on the communication centre installed at the top of Cerro Cacahuatique in southern Morazan. The defence plan for this centre was designed by US military specialists who considered the site to be impenetrable. However, the BRAZ units exploited a weakness and on 31 May, after 20 hours of fighting against a Commando company, the guerrillas took control, seriously disrupting telephone communications in all countries. This action forced the BIRI Atlacatl to suspend its operations in the north of the department to go to the south to rescue the Commandos. Meanwhile, the guerrillas seized Cinquera in the Cabañas department.[5]

The FMLN also struck in the best protected towns. Thus, on 25 May in San Salvador, the number two of the US advisors, the senior US Naval representative Albert Schaufelberger, was assassinated by an urban commando. The event reopened the debate on the presence of American soldiers in El Salvador. On the diplomatic level, the death of Schaufelberger led to the resignation of Thomas Enders, Undersecretary of State for Inter-American Relations, and that of Deane Hinton, US Ambassador to El Salvador.

On 3 June, the FMLN occupied Tenancigo, a small town of 6,000 inhabitants in the Cuscutlan department and attacked seven other towns in three different departments. However, it was the battle for Tenancigo that was receiving international attention. The city was seized over by the FAES but a few days later, the guerrillas stormed it again, crushing the Cazadores battalion which defended it. The FAS bombarded Tenancigo, causing serious damage to the population and numerous civilian casualties. The FMLN exploited this event to make this city the Guernica of El Salvador.[6] If the BIRI Atlacatl reoccupied Tenancigo, the battle for this city was a great propaganda success for the FMLN.

The destruction of the military post at the Quebrada Seca bridge was another success for the guerrillas. The bridge was destroyed and 44 soldiers, who according to the FAES, were killed after surrendering. On 5 June, the explosion of the El Pacayal microwave link complex on the Carrastique volcano, cut the country's telephone links with almost all Central America and isolated the country's four eastern departments.

The FAES did not remain without reaction to the intensification of the actions of the FMLN. On 9 June, the BIRI Atlacatl, led by Monterrosa, advanced towards Agua Blanca with the aim of seizing the ERP headquarters and Radio Venceremos. It was nevertheless, blocked by the guerrillas the next day, which allowed the evacuation of Agua Blanca camp towards Joateca. The soldiers finally reached Cerro Fuero but then suffered night attacks which forced the BIRI Atlacatl to withdraw on 12 June.[7]

US Colonel John D. Waghelstein, Commander of the US Milgroup, played an essential role in the adoption by the FAES of the American counter-insurgency strategy. He designed the National Campaign Plan implemented in the San Vicente department in 1983. (Albert Grandolini Collection)

Operation Bienestar, June – September 1983

As the FMLN began the '*Heroes revolucionarios de enero*' campaign, the FAES launched the '*Bienestar para San Vicente*' operation. The latter was the first to consider US counter-insurgency strategies. On 10 March 1983, Reagan announced that there would be no direct military intervention in El Salvador but only the sending of instructors and military equipment. In accordance with the principles of Low Intensity Warfare, he stated that a military victory would be insufficient to defeat the FMLN without a strategy that sought to win the support of the population through the realisation of civil actions financed by the US Agency for International Development.[8] The message was heard by the command of the FAES.

In June 1983, the FAES adopted an ambitious plan of civic action and pacification, known as the National Campaign Plan (NCP) and designed by, Colonel John Waghelstein, commander of the US Milgroup. By implementing it, the government and the FAES were making a strategic change in the direction desired by the US experts. Moreover, according to one of them, the NCP represented a 'turning point in the war'.[9]

This programme, both military and civilian, aimed to win popular support and regain control of the regions contested by the FMLN. It focused on the sugar-rich regions of the San Vicente and Usulutan departments which the US military believed were the target of FMLN efforts.[10] The first component of the NCP was military; the FAES had to drive out the guerrillas from the areas concerned by sweeps, secure them and leave troops stationed to protect the population. The second phase consisted of carrying out large civic action projects, building hospitals and schools, repairing damaged infrastructure, including power lines, bridges and roads to improve the lives of civilians. Then came the consolidation phase where the FAES handed over control of the area to the local Civil Defence. The importance of this programme lay in the specific weight that the Americans played in its design and its implementation. This was directly linked to political issues since at the end of the year, presidential elections were planned in El Salvador and the transformation of Constituent Assembly to Legislative Assembly.[11]

The Operation Maquilishuat, FAES' largest military offensive since the start of the conflict, inaugurated the NCP and appeared to be a crucial test for the military who had to clear one of the most fertile and partially depopulated, agricultural regions. It started on 11 June 1983 despite the reluctance of the FAES high command and under the supervision of 17 US advisors.

These soldiers installed in the San Vicente department in May 1983 participated in the military success of the FAES during Operation Bienestar para San Vicente. (Albert Grandolini Collection)

Colonel Reinaldo Golcher, who commanded the FAES involved in the operation, systematically used small, highly mobile counter-insurgency battalions. Also participating in the operation were large battalions and airborne forces responsible for saturating the targeted area. The first objective was the encirclement and destruction of FMLN forces in the Chichontepec volcano with 6,000 to 7,000 soldiers and air support. The operation began with the bombardment, by 105mm howitzers, of the guerrillas positions in different areas of the volcano. The soldiers set off for search and destroy operations.[12] Ground operations were coordinated with the Navy, which went up the mouth of the Lempa River to the Amapala bridge. The FMLN choose not to fight and faced with the extent of the encirclement, preferred to abandon its camps.[13]

One hundred days after the launch of Operation Bienestar, the FAES achieved or exceeded all their objectives in the San Vicente department. The second phase of the NCP began with a series of actions to rebuild public services, accompanied by economic development measures and social reforms.[14] All these tasks were coordinated by a newly created body, the National Committee for the Reconstruction of Areas, under the responsibility of Colonel Golcher, head of military intelligence and one of the most valued Salvadoran soldiers in Washington. The operation was directly supervised by US Colonel Peter Stankovich and on 7 September, the US Secretary of Defense, Caspar Weiberger, came to spend a few hours in the San Vicente department.[15]

Nevertheless, the success of the NCP was mixed. Authorities opened 40 schools, enrolled 2,700 people, opened 12 clinics and improved more than 60km of roads. But the Salvadoran government did not have the necessary resources to complete it and at the same time, pursue military operations in the rest of the country. To maintain control in the area seized during Operation Bienestar, the FAES organised Civil Defence units whose main function was to ensure the static security of the region after the departure of the soldiers. However, these poorly armed Civil Defence units were ineffective against the FMLN, whose forces were rapidly returning to the San Vicente department.[16]

The guerrillas were careful to abandon the areas targeted by Operation Bienestar to avoid confronting numerically superior forces, allowing the FAES to occupy the territory without encountering much resistance. Only a month after the start of the operation, the FMLN nevertheless, managed to lay a small ambush in San Vicente. However, it was not until 24 August that it relaunched major operations, reappearing on the Chinchontepec volcano, its traditional refuge in the San Vicente department, forcing the intervention of BIRI Belloso and Atlacatl.

During Operation Bienestar, the FAES did not remain inactive in the rest of the country. Operation Salitre 3 targeted the Cerro de Guazapa from 21 April to 14 May. The soldiers mainly confronted the FARN and the FAR-LP, especially during the battle of El Izcanal where the guerrillas, after a very violent fight, forced the paratroopers to retreat. A pacification operation, like that of San Vicente, was also organised from 4 July, in the south-west and north of the Usulutan department and to a lesser extent, in La Paz department, with the participation of 4,000 men. meanwhile from the 6th, new military operations were launched in Chalatenango and Morazan. It was up to the new Cazadores battalion Lenca, reinforced by two Airborne squadrons, to carry out Operation Morazan five in the north of the department from 4 July to 30 August. It consisted of a series of search and destroy missions in the sectors of Concepcion, Osilaca, Joateca, Perquin, Jocoaitique and San Fernando. The operation was a success for the soldiers who had only three dead and nine wounded.[17]

In Chalatenango department, operations were carried out simultaneously in three directions, while Honduran troops were deployed at the border to prevent the escape of FMLN fighters. The FAES encountered greater resistance here than in San Vicente or Usulutan departments, although the guerrillas only confronted the forces of the 4th Brigade when they were in a good tactical position. The soldiers nevertheless, managed to regain control of part of the territory, in particular the entire northern National Road which connected the country to Honduras.

In the Cabañas department, the presence of the guerrillas was not important but this region was used by its columns as a transit zone between Chalatenango, Morazan and Guazapa areas. Military pressure was maintained there throughout the summer, intensifying at the end of August with Operation Tenancigo 21, in which the FAS, the 1st Brigade and the BIRI Atlacatl (around 2,500 men in total), took part.

FAES soldiers in operation Morazan, 1983. (Albert Grandolini Collection)

Civil Defence units were important in the US counter-insurgency strategy. They had to protect populations and infrastructures against guerrilla incursions. However, their effectiveness was low because they were poorly trained and armed. (Albert Grandolini Collection)

ERP Guerrilla patrol in Jucuaran, August 1983. (Albert Grandolini Collection)

The Military Successes of the FMLN, September – December 1983

From September 1983, the FMLN launched a new offensive, seizing new areas in the eastern third of the country, notably in the San Miguel, Usulutan and Morazan departments. The '*Independencia, libertad y democracia para El Salvador*' campaign began on 3 September with Operation Pedrero, the BRAZ attack on the 3rd Infantry Brigade garrison in San Miguel. This city, 138km east of the capital with 90,000 inhabitants, was the third largest city in El Salvador, an important commercial centre and the seat of the main garrison in the east of the country. The large number of forces used for this action demonstrated the growing military capacity of the FMLN, which brought from the Morazan department, batteries of 81 and 120mm mortars and also 57 and 90mm guns, 75/90mm Recoilless Rifles and M-2 and M-60 machine guns.[18] When it learned of such a movement, the FAES High Command prepared to block the guerrillas by placing a local battalion along the Cerro Cacahuatique. The ERP forces numbered around 1,000 BRAZ men under the command of Jonas. The latter moved a unit to the highlands of Cacahuatique to confront the FAES battalion, which it held for four days, whilst the rest of the forces prepared to storm the San Miguel barracks. The FMLN unit which was to attack the city from the south with 140 men, arrived from the coastal region of Juacarán.[19]

Just before 11:00 a.m. on 3 September, the guerrillas stood ready to launch an artillery attack on the 3rd Brigade as an FES unit infiltrated the base. The 120mm mortars and the 81mm guns were already positioned 1,500 metres from the barracks, the 75mm gun was four blocks away and the .50 calibre machine gun and M-60s were only 400 metres away the target. At 11:00 a.m. the attack began. The soldiers tried to retaliate but the much superior firepower of the FMLN silenced them. The city, defended by a DM-6 infantry company, was quickly defeated with 22 soldiers killed and 70 taken prisoner including two officers. The FAES did not recaptured San Miguel until the evening of the 27th with the help of helicopters which transported paratroopers coming from San Vicente and which united with units of the 1st Infantry Brigade who arrived from Suchitoto.[20]

The FMLN intensified its actions in the region. On 8 September, it seized Jucuaran, whose garrison fled towards Usulutan. On 22 September, the ERP attacked and occupied Nuevo Eden de San Juan north of San Miguel after defeating the Cobra Battalion of DM-2, killing 48 soldiers and capturing seven. On the 25th, the combined forces of FAPL and FAL, captured Tenancingo in the Cuscatlan department, 38km north-east of San Salvador. During the fighting around this city, the FAS massively bombarded it, killing 110 civilians.[21] Nevertheless, the guerrillas prevailed over a Cazadores battalion, of which 80 soldiers surrendered. The same actions were repeated in November in Anamoros with the surrender of a company returning from training in Honduras.

In October, the FMLN tried to regain a foothold between Usulutan and San Miguel, that was to say near the Litoral and Pan-American Highways. Each side occupied and lost villages and towns like Jucuapa, San Buenaventura, Lolotique, El Tránsito.

Whilst the guerrillas had the initiative in El Salvador, the invasion of Grenada by American forces in October 1983 was perceived by the FMLN, but also by the Sandinistas of Nicaragua, as the prelude to direct American intervention in Central America. The FMLN put its forces on alert, improved the defences of the areas it controlled and prepared the campaign '*Yanquis fuera de Granada y de Centroamerica*' which began on 30 October with the siege of Tejutepeque, followed by the occupation of Ciudad Barrios, whose reconquest was entrusted to the BIRI Arce. The FAES then launched, until 10 November, vast operations in the eastern provinces, regaining control of localities in the Usulutan and San Miguel departments. On the 17th, after three days of combat the FAES occupied El Tablon in Morazan department. A new offensive against Guazapa area also provoked heavy fighting around Tenancigo, Suchitoto and Tejutepeque, whilst on the 19th, serious clashes took place in the Cabañas and La Union departments.

In December, various important operations were carried out by the military. The 6th Brigade and BIRI Atonal and Arce acted in the Usulutan department whilst other operations took place in San Miguel and La Paz. Thus, at the beginning of December, the fighting affected all the eastern regions. Once again, the FMLN would hit the FAES hard.

On 14 December, the BRAZ attacked the Cerro Cacahuatique defended by the Tecana Battalion reinforced by a squadron of paratroopers. The attack was combined with other actions launched simultaneously against all military positions within a radius of 50km, which prevented the volcano garrison from being rescued.

In response, the FAES high command decided to undertake a major offensive against the FMLN sanctuaries in Morazan. It wanted to surprise them in their *retaguardia* by landing paratroopers north of San Fernando and near Perquin. meanwhile, the BIRI Atlacatl, Belloso, Arce and the counter-insurgency Cuervo Battalion would advance from San Francisco Gotera to the north and the Pipil Battalion would progress from the east to the north-west to join the paratroopers and form a pincer taking the guerrillas from behind. The operation mobilised 16 UH-1H helicopters, two Hughes-500 armed helicopters, a Cessna O-2A and two A-37B fighter-bombers, as well as a battery of 105mm howitzers to cover the infantry advance.

Salvadoran troops cross the river Torola into guerrilla-held territory. (Albert Grandolini Collection)

The destruction of the Cuscutlan bridge by the FMLN special forces on 1st January 1984 was a severe blow to the FAES. Its international impact demonstrated the operational capabilities of the guerrillas. (Albert Grandolini Collection)

About 2,000 troops began advancing on 20 December. The Atlacatl, Arce, Belloso and Cuervo battalions crossed the Torola River without encountering resistance, seized Meanguera and approached Perquin whilst the paratroopers landed near the border with Honduras, north of San Fernando. The guerrillas were initially surprised, but they reacted and offered a solid resistance which obliged the soldiers to receive the support of A-37 and Hughes-500. The various FAES units then converged on Perquin where the paratroopers were the first to enter on 22 December after hard fighting.

For the next six days, fierce fighting erupted for control of the region. Paratroopers and the Cuscatlan Battalion, supported by 105mm howitzers, fought in the Ciudad Barrios area threatened by ERP attacks. The Cuervo Battalion joined San Miguel before heading to Nuevo Eden de San Juan whilst the BIRI Arce advanced from Perquin towards Carolina, then Sesori and San Gerardo. On 24 December, the Cuervo Battalion was still patrolling the El Trionfo area before receiving the order to withdraw on the 29th. These victories in northern Morazan were nevertheless, quickly eclipsed by a new success for the FMLN.[22]

The Pan-American Highway crossed the Lempa River, which separates the Usulutan and San Vicente departments, by the Cuscatlan bridge, one of the two largest in the country. It was a strategic place, both for the FMLN and for the FAES, since the bridge was the main access route to the east of the country. For the guerrillas, its destruction was an objective that went beyond the strict military framework since it would also be a psychological blow to national and international public opinion.

This mission was entrusted to the ERP whilst the FAPL had to attack the 4th Infantry Brigades garrison in El Paraiso. To destroy the bridge, an operation led by Raul Mijango, FES fighters were sent to Nicaragua to receive special demolition training carried out by the Sandinistas and members of the Basque ETA. The ERP also benefited from the information provided by a deserter from the GN who delivered the plans for the defensive system of the bridge and the composition of the forces defending it. To support the attackers, the guerrillas concentrated two mortars of 120mm, six of 81mm, Recoilless Rifles of 90, 75 and 57mm, that was to say the greatest concentration of artillery of the FMLN during all the war. The Cuscatlan bridge was then defended by 250 men of the GN while patrols of the 3rd and 5th Infantry Brigades monitored the surroundings.[23]

The guerrilla attack was mainly concentrated on the south-east sector of the bridge. Mortar and Recoilless Rifles fire caused many losses among the defenders, which allowed the FES to quickly seize the GN casemate. At the same time, other FES elements moved towards the bridge but were immobilised by the fire of the GN. The guerrilla artillery entered action with efficiency. Saboteurs could approach the bridge and deposit their explosive charges there. The 450m long bridge was destroyed. The guerrillas withdrew without difficulty, to their starting base, the Copalillo camp north of San Miguel with only three wounded.[24]

As the Cuscutlan Bridge collapsed, the FMLN attacked the 4th Infantry Brigade garrison in El Paraiso, a barracks designed by American engineers and deemed impenetrable. This base, one of the newest and most modern, was a sprawling installation that covered one square kilometre. Built on flat land between steep hills to the south, close to the Truncal del Norte Highway, it was about a kilometre and a half, north-east of the town of El Paraiso. A group of FES spent months collecting intelligence and preparing the attack.

The operation was carried out by FPL, FAL and RN forces from San Vicente, Chalatenango and Cerro de Guazapa. Taking advantage of the absence of a significant part of the garrison, in the evening of 28 December 1983, 50 FES covered in mud, dressed only in shorts and carrying German MP-5, Israeli Uzi and American CAR-15 submachine guns (SMG) along with two US M-26 fragmentation grenades, punched several holes in the barbed wire fence and began marking routes through the minefields. Some 300 guerrillas from the FPL's X-21 Battalion, hidden along the outer fence, soon advanced through these paths inside the base. Outside, another FPL battalion K-93 attacked El Refugio, El Barrancon in La Reina and the Colima bridge, to block the relief forces.

The Fuerzas Especiales Selectas formed the FMLN elite units. They distinguished themselves at the end of 1983 with the capture of the El Paraiso barracks on 28 December then the destruction of the Cuscutlan bridge on 1 January 1984. (Author's Collection)

As soon as all resistance was eliminated in the base, the guerrillas, occupying it for another two days, ransacked the installations, gathering useful materials and equipment. Using 3-kilogramme explosive charges, they systematically destroyed buildings, bunkers and heavy equipment. At that time, FAES relief forces, an airborne company and the BIRI Atlatcatl, surrounded the base. The FMLN threatened to kill the soldiers and civilians taken prisoner, forcing the FAES to negotiate. A convoy of 17 trucks and buses from the 4th Brigade was formed to transport the guerrillas, their hostages and the accumulated booty. It was cleared to leave without incident and headed north towards La Palma.[25]

The losses of the FAES were more and more important between 1981 and 1981. Beyond the fighting, it was the mines and traps used by the FMLN, which were the cause of most casualties. (Albert Grandolini Collection)

The attack on El Paraiso killed 400 to 500 soldiers and the 135 prisoners were handed over to the Red Cross in Tejutla. The guerrillas carried 90mm guns, M-60 machine guns. According to the FAES, El Paraiso was the battle where they suffered the greatest number of losses since the beginning of the conflict.[26]

As the Cuscatlan Bridge collapsed and the 4th Brigade base was destroyed, the guerrillas entered Chalatenango, near the barracks, and destroyed the microwave station there. It also seized San Rafael, whose garrison fled. The only failure experienced by the FMLN was

Salvadoran troops training in Panama under the direction of US Special Forces advisors. (Albert Grandolini Collection)

that of the action to destroy the Colima Bridge on 30 December.

The successes of the FMLN seemed irresistible and were reflected in the extension of the territories it controlled. The historian Hugh Byrne wrote, 'According to all indicators – FAES casualties, arms taken, prisoners captured, terrain controlled, major towns and army positions taken, infrastructure damaged or destroyed, level of enemy morale – the guerrillas were winning the war.'[27]

If at the end of 1983, the Salvadoran government avoided defeat, it was far from being able to win on the military ground. Above all, US military advisors doubted that the FAES could overcome their weaknesses. The FMLN still retained the initiative and despite massive US aid, remained a formidable enemy.

The Slow Mutation of the FAES

Despite the ambitious NCP deployed by the FAES and the Salvadoran government, the FMLN was still, at the end of 1983, able to determine the pace of the conflict. 1983 was the year in which the FAES appeared fragile, operating only with conventional forces. The Salvadoran military forces tended to carry out large military operations with the army companies and battalions in search of the guerrillas and their camps. This modality easily allowed the guerrillas to ambush the military and their reinforcements, on the other hand they specialised in night operations, which widened their margin of action since the FAS did not have the capabilities

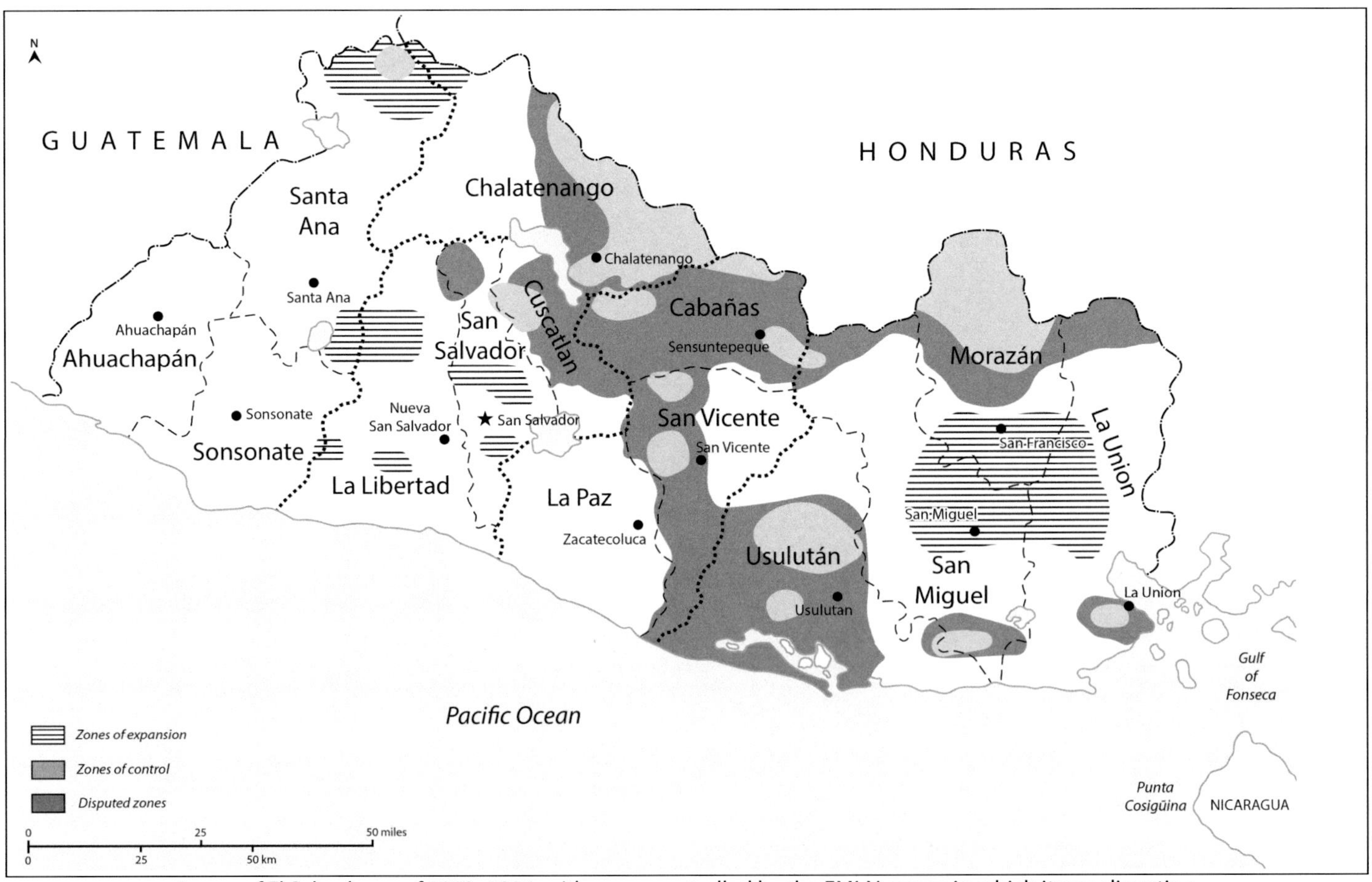

A map of El Salvador as of 1983–1984, with zones controlled by the FMLN, zones in which it was disputing the governmental control and zones into which it was expanding. (Map by George Anderson)

to carry out night operations. Thus, early in the conflict, relatively large rebel columns could even seize and take possession of cities for several days.

The FMLN gained ground, taking control of towns and military posts in the northern, eastern and central regions of the country. It managed to defeat the FAES in major confrontations, to seize some major cities, Berlin in February 1983 and besieged San Miguel, one of the largest cities of the country, in September. The year ended with the successful assault on the El Paraiso barracks and the destruction of the Cuscutlan bridge.

These daring and victorious operations raised fears that the FAES were unable to resist them. This impression was accentuated by the alarming increase in its losses. From 1st July 1982 to 30 June 1983, 2,333 soldiers and 59 officers were killed in action, 4,042 soldiers and 143 officers were wounded and 319 soldiers and nine officers were missing. This represented a 75 percent increase in losses over the previous year.[28]

To the military successes of the FMLN were added those of its sabotage campaign which demoralised the populations of the four eastern provinces. It blew up the Amatillo bridge over the Goascoran River between El Salvador and Honduras on 29 April 1983 and four other bridges between Santa Rosa de Lima and the border. Trade with Honduras was paralysed. The FMLN thus claimed to have carried out, from 1981 to 1983, approximately 2,500 sabotages of electrical installations, transport and communications. The economic deterioration added to the military defeats to further weaken the Salvadoran government. Nevertheless, the year 1983 was also that of the mutation of the FAES.

The soldiers realised that the war would be long and difficult, forcing them to an accelerated accumulation of equipment and human resources. In El Salvador, it fell to the Milgroup, commanded by Colonel Moody E. Hays, to prevent defeat by training the FAES in counter-insurgency tactics. For this, at the end of May 1983, the US and Honduran governments decided to create a Regional Military Training Centre in Puerto Castilla on the Atlantic coast of Honduras. The Centre had 120 US advisors from the 7th Special Forces Group and Green Berets who trained the new BIRI Arce as well as four Cazadores battalions, approximately 2,600 soldiers in 1983. They also used the facilities in Panama, Fort Bragg in Georgia and of Fort Benning in North Carolina.[29] Training centres were also emerging in El Salvador where, between May and June, three new Cazadores battalions were trained and equipped; the Soriano Battalion, the Lenca Battalion in Morazan and the Fonseca Battalion in La Union.[30]

In equipment terms, 1982 was a difficult year for the FAS, which lost seven UH-1Hs, two Lama Sa-315Bs, two Hugues-500Ds and four twin-engine C-47s. These significant losses were nevertheless, quickly compensated by American aid. Thus, at the end of 1982, the FAS had 44 aircraft, including 32 helicopters (five Alouette, three Lama, three Hugues 500D and 21 UH-1H), nine transport planes (four C-47, two Arava and three C-123K), as well as two AC-47s. With these new devices, in 1982 and 1983 it launched a programme of bombardment of villages in the regions held by the FMLN, in particular in Chalatenango department and Cerro de Guazapa.[31]

Thus, under the impetus of the US advisors, the FAES were reorganised to accomplish three main missions. The first was the defence of economic and political areas vital to the government such as bridges, electrical installations or major cities. The second was the organisation of encirclement and destruction campaigns carried out by rapid deployment brigades and battalions. Finally, the last mission was entrusted to mobile, small and self-sufficient battalions, responsible for carrying out counter-insurgency operations using the same methods as the guerrillas. Gradually signs of improvement appeared but American efforts only began to bear fruit in 1984.

CONCLUSION

At the end of 1983, the situation maybe seemed catastrophic for the government of El Salvador. This highlighted the success of the FMLN in a country considered 10 years earlier, as unfit for guerrilla warfare and where the far Left was marginal. In a few years, the latter was able to unify despite its strong differences and build an effective military tool, supported, it was true, by Cuba and Nicaragua. The divisions it knew were even an advantage, as was the case for the Sandinistas before 1979, allowing it strategic flexibility, essential in a long conflict. Thus, after the defeat of its January 1981 offensive and the insurrectional strategy of the ERP, it adopted the strategy of a protracted people's war, concentrating its military action in the east of El Salvador of which it was trying to take control – perhaps to make it a liberated territory, recognised by certain foreign countries or international organisations – more certainly so that it became a starting point to conquer the rest of the country.

Faced with the FMLN, the FAES appeared timorous, unable to adapt to a type of war unknown to them. They nevertheless showed resilience, responding to every action of the guerrillas, recapturing all the important cities lost and preventing them from seizing the east of the country. If this resistance could be explained by the courage of the Salvadoran military, it would have been impossible without American military aid. The formation of counter-insurgency units such as the BIRI and the Cazadores, was driven by US advisors, even if they often came up against the reluctance of the FAES high command. American support rested on a risky bet, that of containing the guerrilla offensives in its *retaguardias*, thus leaving the government the time and the capacity to carry out, in the rest of the country, the economic and political reforms necessary to defeat the FMLN. A bet which, at the end of 1983, seemed on its way to being lost.

SELECTED BIBLIOGRAPHY

Alvarez, Alberto Martin, 'From Revolutionary War to Democratic Revolution. The Farabundo Marti National Liberation Front (FMLN)', in *El Salvador*, Berghof Conflict Research, 2010

Alvarez, Alberto Martin, 'De la guerra revolucionaria a la revolucion democratica. El FMLN en El Salvador', *Revista Realidad*, 132, 2012

Alvarez, Alberto Martin, 'Del partido a la guerrilla: los orígenes de las Fuerzas Populares de Liberacion Farabundo Marti (FPL)', in Juarez Avila, J., *Historia y debates sobre el conflicto armado salvadoreño y sus secuelas*, UES/Fundacion Friedrich Ebert, 2014

Alvarez, Alberto Martin and Cortina Orero, Eudald, 'The Genesis and Internal Dynamics of El Salvador's People's Revolutionary Army, 1970–1976', *Journal of Latin American Studies*, July 2014

Bataillon, Gilles, *Genèse des guerres interne en Amérique centrale, (1960–1983)*, Les Belles Lettres, 2003

Benitez Manaut, Raul Guillermo, *La teoria militar y la guerra civil en El Salvador*, Universidad Nacional Autonoma de Mexico, 1986

Briscoe, Charles H., 'El Paraiso and the War in El Salvador', *Veritas*, vol. 2, no. 3, 2007

Brown, Robert K., 'We can/must win in El Salvador', *Soldiers of Fortune*, July 1983

Cale, Paul P., 'The United States Military Advisory Group in El Salvador', *Small Wars Journal*, 1996

Consalvi, Carlos Enriquez *Broadcasting the Civil War in El Salvador*, University of Texas Press, 2010

Contreras Rodriguez, Marta Elma, *El processo revolucionario en El Salvador*, Universidad Nacional Autonoma de Mexico, 1988

Corum, James S., 'The Air War in El Salvador', *Airpower Journal*, Summer 1998

Crandall, Russell, *The Salvador Option. The United States in El Salvador*, Cambridge University Press, 2016

Crouch, James R., *The Decade of the Seventies in El Salvador: Prelude to Revolution*, Faculty of the US Army and Command and General Staff College, 1992

D'Haeseleer, Brian, *The Salvadoran Crucible: American Counterinsurgency in El Salvador, 1979-1992*, American University, 2015

Escalona Terron, Maria Teresa, *La radio como instrumento de lucha politica: Experiencia de Radio Farabundo Marti, 1982–1992*, Universidad de El Salvador, 2002

Garibay, David *Des armes aux urnes. Processus de paix et réinsertion politique des anciennes guérillas en Colombie et au Salvador*, Institut d'étude politique de Paris-Science Po, 2003

Garcia Fernandez, Anibal, *La presencia militar argentina en El Salvador: el caso del Batallon de Inteligencia 601, (1976-1983)*, Universidad Nacional Autonoma de Mexico, 2017

Giampetri, Sergio M., and Stone Sr, John H., *A Counter Insurgency Study: an Analysis of Local Defenses*, Naval Postgraduate School, 2004

Grenni, Héctor, 'El camino hacia la guerra civil: El Salvador en 1979 y 1980', *Teoria y Praxis*, No 26, January–May 2015

Haggerty, Richard A, (ed.), *El Salvador, a country study*, Library of Congress, Federal Research Division, 1990

Harnecker, Martha, and Villalobos, Joaquin, 'De la insurreccion à la guerra', *Cuadernos Politicos*, no. 35, January–March 1983

Harneker, Marta, *El Salvador: Partido Comunista y guerra revolucionaria. Entrevista a Schafik Jorge Handal, febrero 1985–febrero 1988*, Ediciones Dialectica, 1988

Heigh, Suzanne M., *Counterinsurgency strategies for effective conflict termination: US Strategies in El Salvador*, Naval Postgraduate School, 1990

Hernandez Arias, Miguel, *Fenix, Cenizas de un operacion estadounidense que no renacio*, Centro de Documentacion de los Movimientos Armados, 2006

Hernandez Maldonaldo, Diego Andrés, *Reconstruccion historica de la guerra civil salvadoreña a través de excombatientes del FMLN: caso Guazapa, 1981–1982*, Universidad de El Salvador, 2018

Hone, Matthew James, 'El impacto tactico de la intervencion de EE. UU. en la guerra de El Salvador', *Revista de Humanidades y Ciencias Sociales*, no. 5, July–December 2013

Hone, Matthew James, *La participacion directas de las fuerzas estadounidenses en Centro America durante la guerra fria: el caso de El Salvador*, Universidad Nacional Autonoma de Mexico, 2015

Informe de la Comision de la verdad para El Salvador, *De la locura a la esperanza. La guerra de 12 años en El Salvador*, 1993

International Institute for Strategic Studies, *The Military Balance, 1981–1982*, 1982

Kruijt, Dirk, *Guerrillas. War & Peace in Central America*, Zed Books, 2008

Ladwig III, Walter C., 'Influencing Clients in Counterinsurgency. US Involvment in El Salvador Civil War, 1979–92', *International Security*, vol. 41, no. 1, Summer 2016

Lopez Bernal, Carlos Gregorio, *El Salvador 1960–1992: reformas, utopia revolucionaria y guerra civil, As revoluçoes na America Latina Contemporanea. Entre o ciclo revolucionario e as democracias restringidas*, Pulso & Letra Editores, 2017

Martin-Baro, Ignacio, 'La guerra civil en El Salvador', *Estudios Centroamericanos*, UCA, 1981

Martinez Peñate, Oscar, *El Salvador, el soldado y la guerrillera*, Nuevo Enfoque, 2008

Martinez Peñate, Oscar, *El Salvador del conflicto armado a la negociacion, 1979–1989*, Nuevo Enfoque, 2013

Mauro Araujo, Américo, *Un tiempecito después de terminada la guerra*, Manuscript, 2011

Menjivar Ochoa, Rafael, *Tiempos de Locura. El Salvador, 1979–1981*, FLACSO, 2006

Ministerio de Educacion, *Historia 2, El Salvador*, MINED, 2009

Molinari, Lucrecia I., 'Escuadrones de la Muerte: grupos paramilitares, violencia y muerte en Argentina ('73–'75) y El Salvador ('80)', *Dialogos, Revista Electronica de Historia*, vol. 10, no. 1, February–August 2009

Moroni Bracamonte, José Angel and Spencer, David E, *Strategy and Tactics of the Salvadoran FMLN Guerillas*, Greenwood Publishing Group, 1995

Oñate, Andrea, 'The Red Affair: FMLN-Cuban relations during the Salvadoran Civil War, 1981–92', *Cold War History*, 2011

Paszyn, Danuta, 'The Soviet Attitude to Political and Social change in Central America, Case Studies: Nicaragua, El Salvador and Guatemala', *School of Slavonic and East European Studies*, 1996

Paz Fiumara, Maria, *Exitos y fracasos: las Fuerzas Armadas y de Seguridad en Salvador y Haiti*, CLACSO, 2004

Peña Padilla, Margarita Cecilia, *La Contrainsurgencia en El Salvador*, Universidad Nacional Autonoma de Mexico, 1986

Pettinà, Vanni, *Historia minima de la Guerra Fria en America latina*, El Colegio de Mexico, 2018

Pinkstone, Bobby Ray, *The Military Instrument of Power in Small Wars: The Case of El Salvador*, US Army Command and General Staff College, 1996

Salisbury, Steven, 'Bullets and Ballots. El Salvador From All Sides', *Soldiers of Fortune*, October 1982

Sanchez Ramos, Irene, *Tiempo politico y movimientos armados. El FMLN en El Salvador, 1970–1992*, Universidad Autonoma de Mexico, 1997

Sancho Castañeda, Edoardo, 'El control social y territorial de una fuerza insurgente. El caso de la Resistencia Nacional (RN) durante el conflicto armado', *Revista Policia y Seguridad Publica*, January–June 2016

Schwartz, Benjamin C., *American Counterinsurgency Doctrine and El Salvador. The Frustrations of Reform and the Illusions of Nation Building*, Rand, 1991

Spencer, David E., *From Vietnam to El Salvador. The Saga of the FMLN Sappers and Other Guerilla Special Forces in Latin America*, Praeger, 1996

Sprenkels, Ralph, 'Las relaciones urbano-rurales en la insurgencia salvadoreña', in Jorge Juarez Avila (coord.), *Historia y debates sobre el conflicto armado salvadoreño y sus secuelas*, Institutos de Estudios Historicos, Antropologicos y Arqueologicos, 2014

Tumiatti, Marco, *Reagan's foreign policy and the War Powers Resolution. El Salvador and Nicaragua as test cases of the limits on presidential powers*, Universita Ca'Foscari Venezia, 2019

US Department of States, 'Revolution Beyond our Borders', *Sandinista Intervention in Central America,* September 1983

Valenta, Jiri, *The USSR, Cuba and the crisis in Central America*, Naval Postgraduate School, 1981

Vallenilla, Marianao, *Evolución de la Fuerza Armada de El Salvador en el marco de la ayuda militar brindada por los Estados Unidos de América bajo la presidencia de Ronald Reagan (1981-1989)*, Universidad Catolica Andrés Bello, February 2022

Villalobos, Joaquin, 'Acerca de la situacion militar en El Salvador', *Cuadernos Politicos*, No 30, October–December 1981

Von Santos, Herard, 'Estudio historiográfico sobre los sistemas de inteligencia de los antiguos cuerpos de seguridad pública salvadoreños', *Revista Policia y seguridad publica*, vol. 2, July–December 2015

Von Santos, Herard, 'El Servicio Territorial como parte del sistema de control social y territorial des Estado salvadoreño durante el conflicto armado (1972–1992)', *Revista Policia y Seguridad Publica*, January–June 2016

Von Santos, Herard, *La muerte desde el cielo. La Historia de los Paracaidistas Salvadoreños, 1962–2012*, Tomo I and 2, 2019

Von Santos, Herard, *La Ofensiva Final. El Salvador, 10 enero de 1981*, Circulo de Escritores Militares, 2020

Walker, Greg, 'Blue Badges of Honor', *Soldiers of Fortune*, February 1992

Much of the information can be consulted on various websites and online archives. Many FMLN documents can be consulted on the cedema.org website as well as on marxist.org. Concerning the political and military situation in El Salvador and American policy, hundreds of documents are online on the US Department of State website, foia.state.gov, as well as on the CIA website, cia.gov.

NOTES

Introduction

1 José Angel Moroni Bracamonte and David E. Spencer, *Strategy and Tactics of the Salvadoran FMLN Guerillas*, Greenwood Publishing Group, 1995, p.37.

Chapter 1

1 Richard A. Haggerty (ed.), *El Salvador, a country study*, Library of Congress. Federal Research Division, 1990, p.6.
2 Richard A. Haggerty (ed.), p.7.
3 Rafael Menjivar Ochoa, *Tiempos de Locura. El Salvador, 1979–1981*, FLACSO, 2006, p.142.
4 James R. Crouch, *The Decade of the Seventies in El Salvador: Prelude to Revolution*, Faculty of the US Army and Command and General Staff College, 1992, p.9.
5 Maria Paz Fiumara, Maria Paz Fiumara, *Exitos y fracasos : las Fuerzas Armadas y de Seguridad en Salvador y Haiti*, CLACSO, 2004, p.4.
6 Margarita Cecilia Peña Padilla, *La Contrainsurgencia en El Salvador*, Universidad Nacional Autonoma de Mexico, 1986, p.65.
7 Maria Paz Fiumara, p.5.
8 Ministerio de Educacion, *Historia 2, El Salvador*, MINED, 2009, p.97.
9 James R. Crouch, *The Decade of the Seventies in El Salvador: Prelude to Revolution*, Faculty of the US Army and Command and General Staff College, 1992, p.16.
10 Dirk Kruijt, *Guerrillas. War & Peace in Central America*, Zed Books, 2008, p.22.
11 Rafael Menjivar Ochoa, p.76.
12 Gilles Bataillon, *Genèse des guerres interne en Amérique centrale, (1960–1983)*, Les Belles Lettres, 2003, p.44.
13 Maria Paz Fiumara, p.5.
14 Rafael Menjivar Ochoa, p.78.
15 Richard A. Haggerty, p.18.
16 Rafael Menjivar Ochoa, p.80.
17 Margarita Cecilia Peña Padilla, p.76.
18 Gilles Bataillon, p.56.
19 Margarita Cecilia Peña Padilla, p.78.
20 Richard A. Haggerty (ed.), p.21.
21 Gilles Bataillon, p.100–128.
22 Rafael Menjivar Ochoa, p.188.
23 Carlos Gregorio Lopez Bernal, *El Salvador 1960–1992: reformas, utopia revolucionaria y guerra civil, As revoluçoes na America Latina Contemporanea. Entre o ciclo revolucionario e as democracias restringidas*, Pulso & Letra Editores, 2017, p.244.
24 Bobby Ray Pinkstone, *The Military Instrument of Power in Small Wars: The Case of El Salvador*, US Army Command and General Staff College, 1996, p.10.
25 Carlos Gregorio Lopez Bernal, p.248.
26 Ministerio de Educacion, p.193.
27 Richard A. Haggerty (ed.), p.26.
28 Alberto Martin Alvarez, 'De la guerra revolucionaria a la revolucion democratica. El FMLN en El Salvador', *Revista Realidad*, 132, 2012, p.145.
29 At the end of the 1970s, 40 percent of Salvadoran rural families were landless and according to the United States Agency for International Development (USAID), more than 80 percent of the rural population lived below the poverty line whilst three out of four children under the age of five showed signs of malnutrition. Paradoxically, during these same 1970s, the rate of economic growth was high, on average 4.7 percent per year, but at the same time the population grew faster, from 2.5 million in 1960 to 4.7 million in 1979, Gilles Bataillon, p.103.
30 David Garibay, *Des armes aux urnes. Processus de paix et réinsertion politique des anciennes guérillas en Colombie et au Salvador*, Institut d'étude politique de Paris-Science Po, 2003, pp.240–241.

31 Héctor Grenni, 'El camino hacia la guerra civil : El Salvador en 1979 y 1980', *Teoria y Praxis*, n°26, January–May 2015, p.65.
32 Herard von Santos, *La Ofensiva Final. El Salvador, 10 enero de 1981*, Circulo de Escritores Militares, 2020, p.31. Herard von Santos, a former FAES captain, is the best specialist in the military history of the civil war in El Salvador. His book on the January 1981 offensive is the most comprehensive on the subject, as well as those on the FAES Airborne forces and we rely heavily on them. Herard von Santos is also the author of a blog full of information on the Salvadoran conflict, http://*herard*-elfusilylapluma.*blogspot*.com/.
33 Rafael Menjivar Ochoa, p.134.
34 Margarita Cecilia Peña Padilla, p.86.
35 Dirk Kruijt, p.44.
36 Carlos Gregorio Lopez Bernal, p.254.
37 Herard von Santos, La Ofensiva Final, pp.119–121.
38 Martha Elma Contreras Rodriguez, *El processo revolucionario en El Salvador*, Universidad Nacional Autonoma de Mexico, 1988, p103.
39 Alberto Martin Alvarez, 'From Revolutionary War to Democratic Revolution. The Farabundo Marti National Liberation Front (FMLN)' in *El Salvador*, Berghof Conflict Research, 2010, p.13.
40 Herard von Santos, La Ofensiva Final, pp.145–151.
41 Alberto Martin Alvarez and Eudald Cortina Orero, 'The Genesis ans Internal Dynamics of El Salvador's People's Revolutionary Army, 1970–1976', *Journal of Latin American Studies*, July 2014, pp.670–672.
42 Herard von Santos, La Ofensiva Final, p.33.
43 Gilles Bataillon, p.131.
44 Alberto Martin Alvarez, p.154.
45 Herard von Santos, La Ofensiva Final, pp.156–157.
46 Martha Elma Contreras Rodriguez, p.108.
47 Herard von Santos, La Ofensiva Final, pp.164–166.
48 Dirk Kruijt, p.36.
49 Irene Sanchez Ramos, *Tiempo politico y movimientos armados. El FMLN en El Salvador, 1970–1992,* Universidad Autonoma de Mexico, 1997, p.30.
50 Lucrecia I. Molinari, 'Escuadrones de la Muerte : grupos paramilitares, violencia y muerte en Argentina ('73-'75) y El Salvador ('80)', *Dialogos*, Revista Electronica de Historia, vol. 10, no.1, February–August 2009, p.97.
51 Martha Elma Contreras Rodriguez, p.203.
52 Gilles Bataillon, p.114.
53 *Ibid.* p.97.
54 Russell Crandall, *The Salvador Option. The United States in El Salvador*, Cambridge University Press, 2016, p.57.
55 Héctor Grenni, 'El camino hacia la guerra civil : El Salvador en 1979 y 1980', *Teoria y Praxis*, no. 26, January--May 2015, p.57.
56 Herard von Santos, La Ofensiva Final, p.36.
57 Rafael Menjivar Ochoa, p.27.
58 Alberto Martin Alvarez, p.16.
59 Raul Guillermo Benitez Manaut, *La teoria militar y la guerra civil en El Salvador*, UNAM, 1986, p.275.
60 David Garibay, p.252.
61 Gilles Bataillon, p.232.
62 Alberto Martin Alvarez, p.156.
63 Héctor Grenni, p.61.
64 Gilles Bataillon, p.256.
65 Vanni Pettinà, *Historia minima de la Guerra Fria en America latina*, El Colegio de Mexico, 2018, p.205.
66 Rafael Menjivar Ochoa, pp.25–26.
67 Martha Elma Contreras Rodriguez, p.65.
68 Rafael Menjivar Ochoa, p.113.

Chapter 2

1 Carlos Gregorio Lopez Bernal, p.263.
2 Rafael Menjivar Ochoa, p.200.
3 Walter C. Ladwig III, 'Influencing Clients in Counterinsurgency. US Involvment in El Salvador Civil War, 1979–92', *International Security*, vol. 41, no. 1, Summer 2016, p.111.
4 Rafael Menjivar Ochoa, p.103.
5 *Ibid*. pp.128–130.
6 D'Aubuisson, who was a member of the GN and the Agencia Nacional de Seguridad Salvadoreña (ANSESAL) before leaving the FAES after the Coup of 15 October, was a virulent critic of the reforms and did not hesitate to plot to overthrow the JRG.
7 Richard A. Haggerty (ed.), p.36.
8 Rafael Menjivar Ochoa, p.214.
9 Richard A. Haggerty (Ed.), p.38.
10 Herard von Santos, La Ofensiva Final, p.122.
11 Danuta Paszyn, 'The Soviet Attitude to Political and Social change in Central America, Case Studies: Nicaragua, El Salvador and Guatemala', *School of Slavonic and East European Studies*, 1996, p.138.
12 Herard von Santos, La Ofensiva Final, pp.122–125.
13 Martha Elma Contreras Rodriguez, p.76.
14 Irene Sanchez Ramos, p.76–77.
15 Herard von Santos, La Ofensiva Final, p.43.
16 José Angel Moroni Bracamonte and David E. Spencer, p.3.
17 Andrea Oñate, 'The Red Affair: FMLN-Cuban relations during the Salvadoran Civil War, 1981–92', *Cold War History*, 2011, p.6.
18 David Garibay, p.260.
19 Herard von Santos, *La muerte desde el cielo. La Historia de los Paracaidistas Salvadoreños, 1962–2012*, Tomo I, 2019, pp.203–207.
20 Brian D'Haeseleer, *The Salvadoran Crucible: American Counterinsurgency in El Salvador, 1979–1992*, American University, 2015, p.147.
21 Informe de la Comision de la verdad para El Salvador, *De la locura a la esperanza. La guerra de 12 años en El Salvador*, 1993, p.151.
22 Matthew James Hone, *La participacion directas de las fuerzas estadounidenses en Centro America durante la guerra fria: el caso de El Salvador*, Universidad Nacional Autonoma de Mexico, 2015, p.31.
23 Jiri Valenta, *The USSR, Cuba and the crisis in Central America*, Naval Postgraduate School, 1981, p.19.
24 Herard von Santos, La Ofensiva Final, p.186.
25 Brian D'Haeseleer, p.168.
26 Herard von Santos, La Ofensiva Final, pp.187–189.
27 Russel Crandall, p.176.
28 Jiri Valenta, p.20.

Chapter 3

1 Oscar Martinez Peñate, *El Salvador del conflicto armado a la negociacion, 1979–1989*, Nuevo Enfoque, 2013, p.66.
2 Herard von Santos, La Ofensiva Final, pp.116 and 173.
3 José Angel Moroni Bracamonte and David E. Spencer, pp.5–6.
4 Brian D'Haeseleer, p.184.
5 José Angel Moroni Bracamonte and David E. Spencer, pp.14–16.
6 Rafael Menjivar Ochoa, p.247.
7 Marta Harneker, *El Salvador : Partido Comunista y guerra revolucionaria. Entrevista a Schafik Jorge Handal, febrero 1985–febrero 1988*, Ediciones Dialectica, 1988, p.28.
8 Herard von Santos, La Ofensiva Final, pp.126–128.
9 La Prensa Grafica, *El conflicto en El Salvador*, Dutriz Hermanos, 1992, p.11.
10 Herard von Santos, La Ofensiva Final, pp.136–145.
11 *Ibid*. pp.151–154.
12 Herard von Santos, La muerte desde el cielo, Tomo I, p.273.
13 Herard von Santos, La Ofensiva Final, pp.158–169.
14 Raul Guillermo Benitez Manaut, p.256.
15 Herard von Santos, La Ofensiva Final, p.212.
16 Edoardo Sancho Castañeda, 'El control social y territorial de una fuerza insurgente. El caso de la Resistencia Nacional (RN) durante el conflicto armado', *Revista Policia y Seguridad Publica*, Janvier–Juin 2016, p.200.
17 Richard A. Haggerty (Ed.), pp.242–243.
18 Herard von Santos, La Ofensiva Final, p.175.
19 José Angel Moroni Bracamonte and David E. Spencer, p.18.
20 Dirk Kruijt, 2008, p.84.
21 Russell Crandall, p.52.
22 Herard von Santos, La Ofensiva Final, pp.183–185.
23 José Angel Moroni Bracamonte and David E. Spencer, p.176.
24 Matthew James Hone, p.55.
25 Herard von Santos, La Ofensiva Final, pp.345–352.
26 *Ibid*. pp.192–200.
27 US Department of States, '*Revolution Beyond our Borders*', *Sandinista Intervention in Central America,* September 1983, p.18.
28 Herard von Santos, La Ofensiva Final, pp.201–208.
29 Richard A. Haggerty (ed.), pp.209–210.
30 International Institute for Strategic Studies, *The Military Balance, 1981–1982*, 1982, p.101.
31 Crandall Russell, *The Salvador Option: The United States in El Salvador, 1977–1992,* Cambridge University Press, 2016, pp.176–182.
32 Herard von Santos, La Ofensiva Final, pp.75–80.
33 Sergio M. Giampetri and John H. Stone Sr, *A Counter Insurgency Study: an Analysis of Local Defenses*, Naval Postgraduate School, 2004, p.26.
34 Herard von Santos, *La Ofensiva Final*, pp.443–444.
35 William Green & John Fricker, *The Air Forces of the World*, p.236

36 Inigo Guevara y Moyano, *Latin American Fighters*, pp.150–152
37 For example, see James S. Corum, 'The Air War in El Salvador', Airpower Journal, Summer 1998, p.29; Herard von Santos, *La Ofensiva Final*, pp.95–97; Matthew James Hone, 'El impacto tactico de la intervencion de EE. UU. en la guerra de El Salvador', Revista de Humanidades y Ciencias Sociales, no. 5, July–December 2013, p.134.
38 Russell Crandall, pp.61–62.
39 Paul P. Cale, 'The United States Military Advisory Group in El Salvadore', *Small Wars Journal*, 1996, pp.21–22.
40 Richard A. Haggerty (ed.), p.39.
41 *Ibid.* p.229.
42 Herard von Santos, 'Estudio historiográfico sobre los sistemas de inteligencia de los antiguos cuerpos de seguridad pública salvadoreños', *Revista Policia y seguridad publica*, vol. 2, July–December 2015, p.300.
43 Herard von Santos, La Ofensiva Final, p.113.
44 Dirk Kruijt, p.26.
45 Informe de la Comision de la verdad para El Salvador, p.143.
46 Lucrecia I. Molinari, p.101.
47 Rafael Menjivar Ochoa, p.294.
48 Anibal Garcia Fernandez, *La presencia militar argentina en El Salvador: el caso del Batallon de Inteligencia 601, (1976–1983)*, Universidad Nacional Autonoma de Mexico, 2017, pp.131–135.
49 Matthew James Hone, p.160.
50 Brian D'Haeseleer, pp.116–117.
51 Herard von Santos, La Ofensiva Final, p.109.
52 Brian D'Haeseleer, pp.121–128.
53 Greg Walker, 'Blue Badges of Honor', *Soldiers of Fortune*, February 1992.
54 Herard von Santos, La Ofensiva Final, pp.38 and, 99.
55 Herard von Santos, La muerte desde el cielo, Tomo I, pp.220–228.
56 Carlos Enriquez Consalvi, *Broadcasting the Civil War in El Salvador*, University of Texas Press, 2010, p.XXXI.
57 Herard von Santos, La muerte desde el cielo, Tomo I, pp.231–232.
58 Diego Andrés Hernandez Maldonaldo, *Reconstruccion historica de la guerra civil salvadoreña a través de excombatientes del FMLN: caso Guazapa, 1981–1982*, Universidad de El Salvador, 2018, p.99.
59 Herard von Santos, La muerte desde el cielo, Tomo I, pp.256–263.
60 Herard von Santos, La Ofensiva Final, pp.219–220.
61 Ignacio Martin-Baro, 'La guerra civil en El Salvador', *Estudios Centroamericanos*, UCA, 1981, p.20.

Chapter 4

1 The FMLN called the January Offensive the Final Offensive and, after its failure, the General Offensive.
2 Brian D'Haeseleer, p.152.
3 José Angel Moroni Bracamonte and David E. Spencer, p.17.
4 Rafael Menjivar Ochoa, p.248.
5 Herard von Santos, La Ofensiva Final, pp.231–232.
6 Brian J Bosch, pp.84–85.
7 Herard von Santos, La Ofensiva Final, pp.235–242.
8 Edoardo Sancho Castañeda, p.204.
9 Herard von Santos, La Ofensiva Final, pp.244–248.
10 Brian J. Bosch, pp.84–85.
11 David E. Spencer, From Vietnam to El Salvador. *The Saga of the FMLN Sappers and Other Guerilla Special Forces in Latin America*, Praeger, 1996, pp.47–48.
12 Brian J. Bosch, pp.96–97.
13 Herard von Santos, La Ofensiva Final, p.250–257.
14 Herard von Santos, La Ofensiva Final, pp.263–276.
15 https://elpais.com/diario/1981/01/14/internacional/348274801_850215.html.
16 Herard von Santos, La Ofensiva Final, pp.281–286.
17 *Ibid.* pp.287–294.
18 Carlos Enriquez Consalvi, p.25.
19 Herard von Santos, La Ofensiva Final, pp.297–313.
20 *Ibid.* p.316–319.
21 Brian J. Bosch, p.91.
22 Herard von Santos, La Ofensiva Final, pp.322–323.
23 José Angel Moroni Bracamonte and David E. Spencer, pp.117–118.
24 Herard von Santos, La Ofensiva Final. El Salvador, pp.321–337.
25 *Ibid.* pp.338–345.
26 *Ibid.* pp.376–377.
27 *Ibid.*, pp.357–359.
28 *Ibid.*, p.382.
29 *Ibid.* pp.397–400.
30 Carlos Enriquez Consalvi, p.23.
31 Herard von Santos, La Ofensiva Final, pp.404–420.
32 *Ibid.* pp.435–454.
33 *Ibid.* pp.457–470.
34 Brian J. Bosch, p.88.
35 Herard von Santos, La Ofensiva Final, p.471–475.
36 Raul Guillermo Benitez Manaut, p.301.
37 Herard von Santos, La Ofensiva Final, pp.478–481.
38 Russell Crandall, p.178.
39 José Angel Moroni Bracamonte and David E. Spencer, p.20.
40 Herard von Santos, La Ofensiva Final, p.224.
41 *Ibid.*, pp.493–495.
42 *Ibid.* p.424.
43 Brian J. Bosch, pp.96–97.
44 Brian D'Haeseleer, p.154.
45 Herard von Santos, La Ofensiva Final, p.496.

Chapter 5

1 Brian J. Bosch, p.96.
2 Suzanne M. Heigh, *Counterinsurgency strategies for effective conflict termination: US Strategies in El Salvador*, Naval Postgraduate School, 1990, p.129.
3 Marianao Vallenilla, *Evolución de la Fuerza Armada de El Salvador en el marco de la ayuda militar brindada por los Estados Unidos de América bajo la presidencia de Ronald Reagan (1981–1989)*, Universidad Catolica Andrés Bello, February 2022, p.46.
4 Marco Tumiatti, *Reagan's foreign policy and the War Powers Resolution. El Salvador and Nicaragua as test cases of the limits on presidential powers*, Universita Ca'Foscari Venezia, 2019, p.45.
5 Brian D'Haeseleer, p.172.
6 Paul P. Cale, p.14.
7 Charles H. Briscoe, 'El Paraiso and the War in El Salvador', *Veritas*, vol. 2, no. 3, 2007, p.17.
8 Brian D'Haeseleer, p.171.
9 'The Woerner Report on El Salvador', https://nsarchive2.gwu.edu/nsa/DOCUMENT/930325.htm
10 Brian D'Haeseleer, p.179.
11 Herard von Santos, La muerte desde el cielo, Tomo I, pp.412–413.
12 *Ibid.* pp.7–13 and 383.
13 *Ibid.* p.417.
14 Matthew James Hone, pp.48–49.
15 Dirk Kruijt, p.93.
16 Edoardo Sancho Castañeda, pp.202–207.
17 Carlos Gregorio Lopez Bernal, p.271.
18 Ralph Sprenkels, 'Las relaciones urbano-rurales en la insurgencia salvadoreña', in Jorge Juarez Avila (coord.), *Historia y debates sobre el conflicto armado salvadoreño y sus secuelas*, Institutos de Estudios Historicos, Antropologicos y Arqueologicos, 2014, p.34.
19 Charles H. Briscoe, p.19.
20 La Prensa Grafica, p.31.
21 Brian D'Haeseleer, p.192.
22 Herard von Santos, La muerte desde el cielo, Tomo I, pp.291–306.
23 Diego Andrés Hernandez Maldonaldo, pp.25–27.
24 Herard von Santos, La muerte desde el cielo, Tomo I, pp.307–312.
25 Informe de la Comision de la verdad para El Salvador, p.66.
26 Herard von Santos, La muerte desde el cielo, Tomo I, pp.323–330.
27 Carlos Enriquez Consalvi, p.36.
28 Joaquin Villalobos, 'Acerca de la situacion militar en El Salvador', *Cuadernos Politicos*, n°30, October–December 1981, https://cedema.org/digital_items/7679.
29 Raul Guillermo Benitez Manaut, pp.303–304.
30 Herard von Santos, La muerte desde el cielo, Tomo I, p.346.
31 Maria Teresa Escalona Terron, *La radio como instrumento de lucha politica: Experiencia de Radio Farabundo Marti, 1982–1992*, Universidad de El Salvador, 2002, p.41.
32 Carlos Enriquez Consalvi, p.62.
33 *Ibid.* pp.41–45.
34 Herard von Santos, La muerte desde el cielo, Tomo I, p.348.
35 *Ibid.* pp.354–358.
36 *Ibid.* pp.362–363.
37 Carlos Enriquez Consalvi, p.64.
38 Herard von Santos, La muerte desde el cielo, Tomo I, pp.367–369.
39 Carlos Enriquez Consalvi, p.64.
40 Herard von Santos, La muerte desde el cielo, Tomo I, pp.370–381.

41 Raul Guillermo Benitez Manaut, p.306.
42 Herard von Santos, La muerte desde el cielo, Tomo I, pp.384–389.
43 Marianao Vallenilla, p.100.
44 Carlos Enriquez Consalvi, p.70.
45 Brian D'Haeseleer, pp.193–194.
46 Herard von Santos, La muerte desde el cielo, Tomo I, pp.395–408.

Chapter 6

1 Brian D'Haeseleer, p.199.
2 *Ibid.* p.230.
3 David E. Spencer, pp.49–51.
4 Brian D'Haeseleer, pp.190–191.
5 Herard von Santos, La muerte desde el cielo, Tomo I, pp.424–425.
6 Steven Salisbury, 'Bullets and Ballots. El Salvador From All Sides', *Soldiers of Fortune*, October 1982, pp.48–51.
7 Herard von Santos, La muerte desde el cielo, Tomo I. pp.426–434.
8 Andrea Oñate, p.10.
9 Herard von Santos, La muerte desde el cielo, Tomo I, pp.436–450.
10 *Ibid.* p.457.
11 Brian D'Haeseleer, pp.195–197.
12 Herard von Santos, La muerte desde el cielo, Tomo I, pp.471–472.
13 Carlos Enriquez Consalvi, p.95.
14 Herard von Santos, La muerte desde el cielo, Tomo I, pp.473–477.
15 *Ibid.* pp.479–510.
16 Informe de la Comision de la verdad para El Salvador, p.75.
17 Raul Guillermo Benitez Manaut, pp.316–317.
18 Brian D'Haeseleer, pp.198–199.
19 Herard von Santos, La muerte desde el cielo, Tomo I, p.514.
20 José Angel Moroni Bracamonte and David E. Spencer, p.98.
21 Herard von Santos, La muerte desde el cielo, Tomo I, pp.514–520.
22 *Ibid.*, pp.514–533.
23 *Ibid.* pp.536–542.
24 Ralph Sprenkels, p.34.
25 Herard von Santos, La muerte desde el cielo., Tomo I, pp.542–544.
26 Carlos Enriquez Consalvi, p.100.
27 Herard von Santos, La muerte desde el cielo., Tomo I, p.546.
28 Carlos Enriquez Consalvi, pp.101–103.
29 Herard von Santos, La muerte desde el cielo, Tomo I, p.547.
30 James S. Corum, p.31.
31 Herard von Santos, La muerte desde el cielo, Tomo I, pp.547–549.
32 Raul Guillermo Benitez Manaut, p.320.
33 Herard von Santos, La muerte desde el cielo, Tomo I, pp.549–550.
34 Marta Harnecker, Joaquin Villalobos, https://www.marxists.org/espanol/tematica/elsalvador/villalobos/1982/dic/00a.htm.
35 Informe de la Comision de la verdad para El Salvador, p.130.

Chapter 7

1 CIA, *The Military Situation in El Salvador*, 29 March 1982, p.4, CIA-RDP83M00914R001800010029-5.
2 José Angel Moroni Bracamonte and David E. Spencer, p.71.
3 *Ibid.*, p.57.
4 Miguel Hernandez Arias, *Fenix, Cenizas de un operacion estadounidense que no renacio*, Centro de Documentacion de los Movimientos Armados, 2006, p.21.
5 The FMLN had a significant proportion of women, estimated at 30 percent among the rank and file fighters and 20 percent among the command, which made the Salvadoran guerrillas one of the most feminised in Latin America, David Garibay, p.557.
6 José Angel Moroni Bracamonte and David E. Spencer, p.74.
7 Herard von Santos, La muerte desde el cielo, Tomo II, pp.69–71.
8 Herard von Santos, La muerte desde el cielo, Tomo I, pp.550–553.
9 Marta Harnecker, Joaquin Villalobos, https://www.marxists.org
10 Herard von Santos, La muerte desde el cielo, Tomo I, pp.553–554.
11 David E. Spencer, p.82.
12 Herard von Santos, La muerte desde el cielo, Tomo I, pp.556–560.
13 Herard von Santos, La muerte desde el cielo, Tomo II, p.26.
14 Marta Harnecker, Joaquin Villalobos, https://www.marxists.org.
15 Maria Teresa Escalona Terron, p.48.
16 Robert K. Brown, 'We can/must win in El Salvador', *Soldiers of Fortune*, July 1983, p.83.
17 Brian D'Haeseleer, p.212.
18 Herard von Santos, Tomo I, pp.561–562.
19 Herard von Santos, La muerte desde el cielo, Tomo I, pp.550–555.
20 Matthew James Hone, p.100.
21 Herard von Santos, La muerte desde el cielo, Tomo II, p.46.
22 Carlos Enriquez Consalvi, p.113.
23 Herard von Santos, La muerte desde el cielo, Tomo II, p.17.
24 Carlos Enriquez Consalvi, p.130.
25 José Angel Moroni Bracamonte and David E. Spencer, pp.104–105.
26 Carlos Enriquez Consalvi, p.131.
27 Herard von Santos, La muerte desde el cielo, Tomo II, pp.46–48.
28 Herard von Santos, Tomo II, pp.17–18.
29 Herard von Santos, La muerte desde el cielo, Tomo II, pp.20–26.
30 *Ibid.* pp.37–43.

Chapter 8

1 Alberto Martin Alvarez, p.178.
2 Rafael Menjivar Ochoa, pp.57–59.
3 Martha Elma Contreras Rodriguez, pp.135–136.
4 Carlos Enriquez Consalvi, pp.138–139.
5 Herard von Santos, La muerte desde el cielo, Tomo II, p.48.
6 Carlos Enriquez Consalvi, p.141.
7 *Ibid.* p.142.
8 Rafael Menjivar Ochoa, p.57.
9 Brian D'Haeseleer, p.215.
10 Charles H. Briscoe, p.19.
11 Benjamin C Schwartz, *American Counterinsurgency Doctrine and El Salvador. The Frustrations of Reform and the Illusions of Nation Building*, Rand, 1991, p.51.
12 Herard von Santos, La muerte desde el cielo, Tomo II, p.63.
13 Raul Guillermo Benitez Manaut, pp.344–345.
14 Brian D'Haeseleer, p.219.
15 Herard von Santos, La muerte desde el cielo, Tomo II, p.64.
16 Brian D'Haeseleer, pp.219–220.
17 Herard von Santos, La muerte desde el cielo, Tomo II, pp.31–50.
18 *Ibid.*, p.66.
19 David E. Spencer, pp.83–84.
20 Herard von Santos, La muerte desde el cielo, Tomo II, p.68.
21 Informe de la Comision de la verdad para El Salvador, p.27.
22 Herard von Santos, La muerte desde el cielo, Tomo II, pp.72–75.
23 David E. Spencer, pp.85–86.
24 Herard von Santos, La muerte desde el cielo, Tomo II, pp.76–83.
25 Charles H. Briscoe, pp.16–21.
26 Brian D'Haeseleer, p.219.
27 Walter C. Ladwig III, p.126.
28 Herard von Santos, La muerte desde el cielo, Tomo II, p.56.
29 Matthew James Hone, p.79.
30 Herard von Santos, La muerte desde el cielo, Tomo II, p.61.
31 James S. Corum, p.32.

ABOUT THE AUTHOR

David François, from France, earned his PhD in Contemporary History at the University of Burgundy and specialised in studying militant communism, its military history and relationship between politics and violence in contemporary history. In 2009, he co-authored the Guide des archives de l'Internationale communiste published by the French National Archives and the Maison des sciences de l'Homme in Dijon. He is regularly contributing articles for various French military history magazines and is a regular contributor to the French history website *L'autre côté de la colline*.